REVISED EDITION

SUPER POWER GOLF

Techniques for Increasing Distance

DR. GARY WIREN
PGA Master Professional
with Dawson Taylor

Foreword by Gary Player

CB
CONTEMPORARY BOOKS

Library of Congress Cataloging-in-Publication Data

Wiren, Gary.
    Super-power golf : techniques for increasing distance / Gary
Wiren with Dawson Taylor.—Rev. ed.
       p.   cm.
    Includes index.
    ISBN 0-8092-2919-6
    1. Golf.   2. Swing (Golf)   3. Golf—Drive.   I. Taylor,
Dawson.   II. Title.
GV965.W73   1998
796.352'3—dc21   97-32414
                                        CIP

Cover design by Todd Petersen
Cover photograph by Carlisle Photography, Inc.
Interior design by Hespenheide Design

Published by Contemporary Books
An imprint of NTC/Contemporary Publishing Group, Inc.
4255 West Touhy Avenue, Lincolnwood (Chicago), Illinois 60646-1975 U.S.A.
Copyright © 1984, 1998 by Gary Wiren and Dawson Taylor
All rights reserved. No part of this book may be reproduced, stored in a retrieval
system, or transmitted in any form or by any means, electronic, mechanical,
photocopying, recording, or otherwise, without the prior permission of
NTC/Contemporary Publishing Group, Inc.
Printed in the United States of America
International Standard Book Number: 0-8092-2919-6

15   14   13   12   11   10   9   8   7   6   5   4   3   2   1

Contents

Foreword   v

Introduction   vii

Coauthor's Statement   xi

1 There Is No *One* Perfect Golf Swing   1

2 The Foundations of a Power Golf Swing   11

3 Training and Exercises   61

4 Equipment   97

5 Driving for Distance   113

6 The World's Longest Hitters   139

7 Random Insights and Selected Observations   153

  Index   163

Foreword

Without special physical conditioning, I could never have competed as successfully as I have in my career. This becomes particularly true now that I have reached senior status. Personally, I enjoy working out. For those who haven't experienced the joy of being in condition, I'd strongly recommend it for a happier life, not to mention for better golf.

I've been with thousands of amateurs in Pro-Am competition and have observed their play. Most could have improved their ability to swing simply by improving their level of fitness. Lack of flexibility and strength limits so many players from reaching their golf potential, especially seniors and ladies.

That is why I'm happy to see my friend Gary Wiren offer this book on adding length to your game. Because he recognizes as I do the importance of the condition of the human body in producing consistently good golf shots, I couldn't agree more with Gary that "training for golf" is one of the next movements in golf that a serious player will incorporate to improve his or her game. I most heartily endorse that concept and encourage you to participate. You'll see the difference in your performance.

GARY PLAYER

Introduction

If you want to hit a golf ball farther than you do now regardless of your age, handicap level, or physical condition, this book can help you do it. That's not just a lightly considered promise. It's a statement based upon my study of the power golf swing for many years and my experience in applying that knowledge to my own swing and the swings of thousands of other golfers.

I am Gary Wiren, 62 years of age, the former National Director of Learning and Research for the Professional Golfers' Association of America. I am a PGA Master Professional and have taught golf to more than 300,000 people in 26 countries. I have a doctorate in physical education. My doctoral dissertation was written on "Human Factors Influencing the Golf Drive for Distance." So you can readily understand my interest and why, for more than 40 years, I have been concentrating on the solution to the problem of driving a golf ball farther.

At 5 feet 11 inches and 185 pounds, I am not a "gorilla." But as you will discover in reading this book, I am reasonably strong as a result of an exercise program that I have conscientiously carried out for many years.

In the 1983 National Long Drive Competition, I won, at the age of 47, the local qualifying round with a hit of 381 yards, 1 foot. That shot was 50 yards beyond the nearest of my 83 competitors! It was most satisfying to realize that at that age in my life I could accomplish such a feat. I am still learning new things about my swing, working on it, and improving it. That is the underlying theme of this book. If I can do it, you can do it too, if you want to badly enough. We are going to show you how.

I have always been fascinated by physical feats that require great strength. It has amazed me that people could drive spikes into boards with their bare hands, lift gargantuan weights from the floor, bend bars of metal, or pull a row of railroad cars along a track. The act of hitting a golf ball a prodigious distance appears to be just as awe-inspiring to a multitude of golfers. After all, driving a golf ball 300 to 350 yards is a physical accomplishment that should not go unrecognized. It requires a golf clubhead to be traveling some 140 mph and produces thousands of pounds of force at impact.

Performers of great feats of strength generally stand out from the crowd physically. They are usually extremely muscularly endowed or, if they lack muscle definition, have massive bulk that disguises their power. This is not necessarily true in the case of golfers. Some of the longest hitters in the world have not been large people. Before his automobile accident in 1952, Ben Hogan, at 5 feet 7 inches, 145 pounds, was the winner of many long drive contests. So was Juan "Chi Chi" Rodriguez at 5 feet 6 inches, 138 pounds. Anyone can understand how a generation ago George Bayer, at 6 feet 5 inches, 255 pounds, was a long hitter, but how does one explain how the smaller people can perform equally well?

When I started looking more closely at the matter back in the mid-1960s, it seemed as though the golf literature offered a variety of explanations. When they were interviewed on the subject of distance, great players made different remarks. Tommy Armour talked about hands as his source of power, Bobby Jones his timing, and Jack Nicklaus his legs. The fact is that there is no one set of muscles or a single movement that is responsible. It is a combination of factors that work to create distance—with each individual emphasizing his or her own particular strengths.

At the age of 13 I attended my first golf clinic at a dirt tee public course in Omaha, Nebraska, where an honest-to-goodness PGA professional (the first one I'd ever seen) was giving the lesson. The teacher was a proper Englishman, who still played in knickers and possessed one of those classic "turn in a barrel" swings that produced a beautiful repeating draw. Unfortunately, his drive traveled only about 225 yards after its roll. When he finished his demonstration he asked some of us "kids" in the gallery to give it a try. I accepted the challenge and stepped up to the tee. With my ugly caddy grip, closed stance, and overswing, I caught a beauty that drove the ball about 20 yards past his. *"That's not the way you do it,"* was the next line I heard—and I was summarily dismissed in favor of a shorter hitter. I smile now as I recall that incident because the attitude toward instructing young players today is more to: *"Teach them to hit it a long way; and when they've learned that, we'll teach them to hit it straight."*

There is no question that heredity plays a large part in your present ability or potential ability to drive the golf ball for distance. Who could argue otherwise? But how about getting the most out of what you have? The development of sound technique and the maintenance and strengthening of your body are two of the critical factors that will influence your ability to reach your potential. That's all any of us can hope to do.

Let me give you a couple of examples of different approaches that accomplished the same result. I put one college underclassman on a training program that included a specially constructed, progressively weighted driver. Within two years he won the NCAA Long Drive Contest. Another one of my pupils, a reasonably long driver after improving her mechanical technique, added an additional 20 yards to her tee shots through an intensive course on machine weight training equipment. The interesting part of her story is that when she interrupts her training regime for any period of time, her club control and distance both diminish noticeably.

You will be given a complete training program in this book. You may not wish to do all the exercises; you may not have the time to do them. But even if you select a part of the program that you can fit into your life—just 20 minutes, three times a week—I promise you that you will see a noticeable difference in the length of your drives in the future.

Golf's "golden steps" are those you take when you walk past your opponent's drive. You'll be taking them more often if you read and practice the material in this book.

GARY WIREN

Coauthor's Statement

Several years ago, after I had struggled with long drives for my entire golf-playing career, Gary Wiren shared with me his advice and exercises for increasing my distance. He explained how important it was that through exercise I increase the arc of my swing, get a better turn, and be able to retain the hit until later in my swing. I took his advice about the exercises and faithfully carried out a regime of stretching and using a heavy golf club.

The results of this long campaign to increase my driving distance were most satisfying. For a number of years there wasn't a single long four-par at my home course, Atlantis Golf Club, that I could not reach in two strokes.

This leads me to feel that I "fathered" this book. I realized what Gary Wiren had done for my driving ability and told him many times that he should write this book so he could help other golfers the way he helped me.

At last he agreed to write it provided I helped him find the time to put it together. Most gladly I agreed. The book in your hands is the pleasant result.

One final statement. This is Gary Wiren's book on how to drive the golf ball a long, long way. The "I" speaking represents the thoughts and voice of Gary Wiren.

I sincerely hope the book will add as much to your enjoyment of golf as the ideas in it have added to mine.

DAWSON TAYLOR

"Anything you can do to improve your overall
physical condition will benefit your play."

BOB TOSKI AND JIM FLICK

1
There Is No *One* Perfect Golf Swing

Man has always been fascinated by the challenge of the unknown, the resolutions of apparently insoluble problems, some worthy, some capricious. One persistent enigma that has tantalized the minds and tested the skills of golfers since the 17th century has been the search for the *perfect golf swing*—particularly one that combines accuracy with power.

Hundreds, possibly thousands, of devotees of the game have invested their time and talent toward this rewarding goal, but no one man has dedicated his enthusiasm and financial resources in such a grand manner as did the English gentleman Sir Ainsley Bridgland. Wealthy in his own right, a keen golfer, and of questioning mind, Sir Ainsley had a haunting feeling that there must be some hidden secret in the game of golf, some simple key that would unlock for him and possibly for all golfers the treasure house of the perfect swing. Certainly, he reasoned, if the swing were carefully studied under controlled conditions with the latest in engineering aids like high-speed photography, the secret would be revealed. That is precisely what he set out to do.

With the cooperation of the Golf Society of Great Britain, Bridgland sponsored the formation of a first-rate team of specialists representing many different disciplines: biomechanics, engineering, anatomy, physiology, ballistics, medicine, physical education, and ergonomics (the application of engineering data to problems relating to the adjustment of man and the machine). Needless to say, Bridgland believed that with a team such as he had assembled, the answer to his quest would inevitably be found.

The team of experts experimented, discussed, and analyzed the various elements of the game of golf for more than five years. The results of their work culminated in the publication in 1968 of the most fascinating technical book ever written on the golf swing. The authors were physicist/author Alistair Cochran and golf writer John Stobbs. The book was called *The Search for the Perfect Swing*.

Unfortunately for Bridgland and for all golfers, the search for a particular "secret" of the golf swing was not successful. The reams of experimental test data, mathematical models, hypotheses, computer printouts, and high-speed camera work did not provide Bridgland with the answer he wanted. The conclusion of all the studies, on the other hand, was this: although a model can be constructed that exemplifies sound principles in the golf swing, *there is no one perfect golf swing* for all. The idea of there being a single perfect swing for distance or direction that fits everyone is a myth. Instead, the conclusion was that there are many variables that are functional and can be considered correct as long as they do not violate physical law. That is why you see a variety of swing styles among the greatest players in the world. It is also one of the reasons why there is a variety of opinion about why some people can produce prodigious drives and others can't.

There must be individualism in swinging a golf club. However, such individualism can never give license to employ a technique that violates physical law or basic principle. For example, it would be wrong to teach golfers to use a grip with both hands facing the sky, because such a grip would restrict angular motion and leverage in the swing. That grip might be very effective for putting or even chipping, where maximum clubhead velocity is not a factor, but it would violate physical principle if it were applied to the full golf swing.

Even a casual study of the game's greatest performers should convince the most stubborn advocate of a single swing style that individual differences do exist. The only absolute statement you can make about the swings of great golfers is that they all are different. Many are similar looking, I'll agree. All those good swings share a common ground in principle. But no two swings are exactly the same. I believe that recognizing the individual differences in students raises teaching to an art. So let's discuss a teaching model that recognizes those differences, one in which method does not overpower or replace result.

This proposed model offers three levels of priority in understanding the golf swing and helps to explain the causative factors in producing distance. Those levels of priority are:

1. Laws
2. Principles
3. Preferences

Each is defined in the following manner:

Law—A statement of an order or relation of phenomena that, so far as is known, is invariable under given conditions. It refers to the dynamic characteristics of the clubhead and ball at the moment of energy transfer that directly influence the flight of the ball.

Principle—A first cause, or primary force. It is a factor of high order that must be dealt with and which, in this model, has direct relation to and influence on *law*. Some call it a fundamental.

Preference—The act of choosing and liking better some particular style, method, or device over all others. To be valid in this model, it must relate to *principle*.

THE BALL FLIGHT LAWS

The Ball Flight Laws in this model, assessed at the moment of impact (along with the primary result), are:

1. Speed—The velocity at which the clubhead is traveling influences the distance the ball will be propelled.
2. Centeredness—The point on the clubface where the ball is struck will influence distance and direction.
3. Path—The direction in which the clubhead is moving will influence the direction in which the ball will travel.
4. Face—The degree at which the surface of the clubface, running on a horizontal axis, is at right angles to the swing line will influence the accuracy of the ball's flight.
5. Angle of Approach—The steepness of the descent or ascent of the clubhead in the forward swing will influence the trajectory and the distance the ball will travel.

Ball Flight Laws are the most important because they work every time without fail. The ball is not concerned with the technicalities of swing style. It responds to being struck without any prejudice toward the striker. It doesn't ask what particular swing method is being used, nor does it care about handicap, club affiliation, sex, or age. It follows the basic Ball Flight Laws, whether the golfer uses an open or square stance, has a firm or cupped wrist, or uses leverage or centrifugal force as his or her primary source of power.

Obviously, there are equipment factors such as clubface loft, construction of the ball, and material of the hitting surface that will influence distance and direction of the ball's flight. Environmental conditions such as temperature, humidity, wind, terrain, and altitude are also recognized as having an effect. In this book, however, we consider only the physical human factors over which we have some control.

PRINCIPLES OF THE SWING

The aforementioned five factors determine the flight of the ball. But there are fundamental technique elements in the swing that have a direct bearing on a player's application of the Laws and therefore influence distance and direction to some degree. They are called *Principles of the Swing*. Whereas the Laws are irrefutable and absolute (at least as absolute as we can be in this relative universe), the Principles reflect subjective judgment on the mechanics of the swing. Listing these elements does not mean the list is all-inclusive. The Principles are divided into two categories: Pre-Swing and In-Swing.

Pre-Swing Principles

1. **GRIP:** Grip has a significant influence on several of the Ball Flight Laws but primarily the face position. Rotation of the hands less than one-half inch clockwise in the grip can cause the clubface to open enough for a 40-yard slice. A 40-yard off-line shot can cause the player to attempt adjustments in other parts of the swing.
2. **AIM:** One of the principles that is violated most frequently and often unknowingly by the golfer, *aim* includes both aim of the clubface and aim of the body. Proper body aim, or alignment, has a strong influence on proper path, though it does not guarantee it.
3. **SETUP** (includes posture, ball position, stance, and weight distribution): Setup influences all five of the Ball Flight Laws: clubhead speed, clubhead path, position of clubface, angle of approach, and centeredness of contact. Ball position, for example, affects the angle of clubhead approach and trajectory of the shot. A ball played forward in the stance will tend to increase the clubface angle at impact, resulting in a higher shot. A ball played back in the stance

has the opposite result. There are similar examples for each segment of setup.

In-Swing Principles

1. **DOWNSWING PLANE** (the angle of tilt the shaft makes toward the player in the forward swing; a flat plane would be closer to horizontal, an upright plane closer to vertical): The downswing plane is measured by the position of the clubshaft. It is said to be *in plane* and therefore correct when, midway through the downswing, an extension of the butt end of the club would intersect a line drawn through the ball to the target line. If the butt end of the club points outside (to the right of) the intended flight line, the clubhead will travel from inside to outside. If it points inside (to the left), the swing will be from outside to inside.

2. **LEFT WRIST POSITION** (the relationship between the back of the left hand and the back of the left forearm): By cupping (concave) or arching (convex) the left wrist, the clubface position can be dramatically influenced. Cupping opens the face, and arching closes it. Mechanically, the simplest method is to allow the wrist to cock, but in a plane that keeps the left hand and wrist in a flat plane throughout the swing. This, however, is not always desirable, comfortable, or even physically possible for many golfers. The player's grip will strongly influence the position at the top of the swing and will determine which position the wrist should seek. The objective is to assume a square clubface position so no manipulation will be required on returning to the ball.

3. **WIDTH OF ARC** (the radius or distance from the center of the swing to the clubhead): If the golfer allows his left arm to bend before impact, his clubhead speed is reduced because the lever length is shortened. It is this same principle that causes the middle portion of a spoke on a wheel to travel more slowly than the far end of the spoke even though the force emanating from the axle is the same.

4. **LENGTH OF ARC** (the distance the clubhead travels in degrees from address to the completion of the backswing and then to the follow-through): Limiting the length of the backswing in the short game basically limits the distance the ball will travel. For example, consider the length of the backswing for a short putt and contrast it to that of a 20-yard pitch shot. The longer backswing obviously produces more potential for distance. In the full swing this is true as well, up to a point. Taking the club back too far can cause loss of control, but the reverse, too short a backswing, is the more common problem.

5. **LEVER SYSTEM*** (the series of levers in the body in combination with the club, which transmits energy through muscular and mechanical action): A swing without cocking the wrist, such as in a chip shot, is referred to as a one-lever swing. Adding a second lever by cocking the wrists allows the golfer to markedly increase his or her potential force in the full swing.

6. **TIMING** (the order in which physical movements of the body and club happen during the swing): The backswing should occur in this order: (1) hands and arms, (2) shoulders, (3) trunk, (4) hips and legs, and (5) feet. The forward swing should return in reverse of this sequence, with the arms bending during the forward motion and hands firing last. When this sequence occurs, the greatest possible force is unleashed.

7. **RELEASE** (allowing the hands, arms, and clubface to naturally return from the top of the backswing and the energy created in the backswing to be delivered to the ball): The momentum of the club encourages the arms and hands to make a natural release when the ball is struck. Proper release can be inhibited if there is undue muscular tension. Conscious attempts to hit hard can cause hand and forearm tension or disturb the timing of a natural release, inhibiting a return to square.

---

*Actually, there are several systems of levers operating in the golf swing. The primary one referred to in this model is that formed by the left arm and the club. When the arm is extended, there is a single lever, but when the wrist cocks, the result is a two-lever system.

8. **DYNAMIC BALANCE** (the ability to transfer the body weight during the swing from a static position to a positive, energy-creating moving force while still maintaining body control): Nearly all good players use the footwork common to striking and throwing actions, that is, moving from the back to the front foot in delivering the blow. Remaining on the back foot reduces the power of the swing and changes the desired path. Failure to get the weight over the rear leg on the backswing reduces the player's power.

9. **SWING CENTER** (that point in the body around which the body's rotation is made; located between the shoulders at the top of the spine): Technically, the golf swing is an ellipse, but it is close to being a circle. When the rotational swing center is moved, the arc of the circle moves, and striking the ball consistently is extremely difficult.

10. **CONNECTION** (keeping the club and body parts in the proper relationship to one another, both at address and during the swing): When one part of the body gets markedly out of position or out of sequence in relation to its adjoining part, it is said to be disconnected. It can happen at address (by reaching too much for the ball) or during the swing (lifting the arms excessively at the top of the backswing). When staying connected, the elements of the body and club that produce the swing stay in their correct relationship and sequence during the swing.

11. **IMPACT** (the moment of truth when the club and ball collide and the energy is transferred to send the ball on its way): All the principles affect Impact, but Impact is the only principle that directly influences the ball. Thus, I'd call it the Master Principle.

PREFERENCES

The final level of fundamentals is the most practical, because it is the level on which we most often operate. It is labeled *Preferences*, or choices in style. For example, under the Principle of Setup, the choices of open, closed, or square stance; wide or narrow foot position; and weight on heels or toward toes are all viable possibilities. There are literally thousands of combinations.

Example A

Let's put all three levels together.

Law: *Speed.*

Principle: *Two-Lever System.* When you transfer from a one-lever system (which would occur if you tried to swing the golf club with no wrist cock) to a two-lever system created by the left arm and club as the wrist is cocked, you multiply the potential force by an additional 50 to 60 percent.

Preference: If you need more than one lever in the arm and club relationship, the question is where should you create this second

The body is behind the ball in the backswing, weight over the right leg, ready to deliver energy. The two levers are the left arm and the club.

lever, or where should you cock your wrist? Early? In midswing? At the top of the swing? On the downswing? Or even before you start the backswing, in a pre-set fashion? That's a *preference*.

Example B

Law: *Squareness.*

    Principle: *Grip.*

    Preference: Should the pupil use a three-knuckle visible grip in the left hand? Two-knuckle? Overlapping? Interlocking? Full-fingered? Cross-handed? Should there be strong pressure? Light pressure? Again, the answers will depend on the individual. Some experimentation might be necessary to find the right combination of grip elements that will produce the desired ball flight.

    When you consider the Preference category, the possibilities are limitless. Examine the preferences you find in many excellent golf swings. Consider the following: Should the shoulders be aimed to the left, to the center, or to the right of the target? Should the stance be open, square, or closed? Should the weight be back or forward at address? Should the left or right side be favored? Is the ball position variable or constant? Should the body at address be relaxed or taut? Is it a flat, medium, or upright plane? Is the left arm bent or straight at the top of the backswing? Is the backswing short or long? Is the left wrist cupped, flat, or arched?

    Is the face open, square, or shut to the tangent of the arc? Is the swing-through initiated with the feet, knees, legs, hips, arms, or hands? Is the hip movement lateral, circular, or both? Do the forearms rotate to provide release, or is it the wrists, or both? Where is the weight distributed during the swing? Does the left knee straighten on the downswing or stay flexed? Does the head move laterally, up, or down? Whereas the Laws are fixed in number, and the Principles are limited, the Preferences reach a staggering total. The point is that there are a great many techniques and combinations of techniques that can work and do work. One objective of this book is to help you find the right ones that will give you the most functional power.

"The day of the short hitter is gone. No longer can a player who drives the ball 250 yards—or less—be one of the world's best for very long at a time. Length and strength are the necessary ingredients for the world class player of the future. . . . That's why our fitness trainers are busier than ever; [Tiger] Woods is in the weight room probably four times a week. No wonder he's so strong and flexible."

CURTIS STRANGE, TWICE U.S. OPEN CHAMPION

2
The Foundations of a Power Golf Swing

THE WHOLE PICTURE

I like to think of the golf swing as a jigsaw puzzle in motion. We all know that no jigsaw puzzle is complete until the last piece is inserted into the overall picture. We also know that if any one piece of the puzzle is missing, the picture will never be completed satisfactorily.

The principle of the jigsaw puzzle applies as well to the golf swing. It is put together with many separate pieces or elements, and yet when all of the parts come together properly the result is a smooth, rhythmic, effective, and powerful golf swing—the completed picture.

In the following chapters we will focus on the individual parts of the golf swing, but you must not conclude that the swing is a disjointed mixture of many separate pieces or movements. It is not. An automobile engine is made of many working parts, but when they are all put together properly the result is a single entity, a well-functioning machine that delivers power smoothly to the wheels of a car. We can examine closely a particular part of a car engine, such as the function of a piston, without losing sight of the fact that it is merely an important, vital part of the complete engine. In the same way, we propose to examine the parts of the golf swing. When they are understood and assembled intelligently, they result in the completed jigsaw puzzle—a golf swing that is efficient, repeating, and powerful enough to drive a golf ball a great distance.

THE PROPER GRIP

There has been a great deal of discussion and even controversy for many years over the proper way to grip a golf club. You have heard golfers talk of the overlapping or Vardon grip, the baseball grip, the interlocking grip, and about "strong" and "weak" positions of the hands. It is most important that you understand the basic elements of each one of these grips so that you can make your own decision about the way you should grip the golf club most effectively and swing it with the greatest efficiency and power.

Early photographs of golfers of the 1800s tell us that they held the golf club with both hands positioned similarly to the way an ordinary person would grip an axe. In other words, they held the handle in the palms with no locking or overlapping of the fingers but the hands held as close together as possible. It was obvious even in the early days of golf that the closer the hands, the more the "hit" at the golf ball was a unified effort, that is, one in which neither hand was more in control of the swing than the other at the moment of striking.

Then, in the 1890s, a great golf champion, John Henry Taylor (a Scotsman who was always called "J.H."), made a discovery while playing with an amateur, J. E. Laidlay. Taylor found that if he copied Laidlay's grip by overlapping the little finger of his right hand with the forefinger of his left hand, he could achieve consistently more compactness in his grip. Another great golfer of that day, Harry Vardon, who competed frequently with Taylor, adopted Taylor's new grip idea, and when Vardon won tournament after tournament using it, the public began to call the grip the "Vardon grip." To this day, it is probably the grip most universally used by golfers. But it was created by an amateur, Mr. Laidlay.

There are notable exceptions from those who use the Vardon style. The most prominent nonuser of the Vardon grip has been Jack Nicklaus, who does not have large hands. Nicklaus, along with Phil Mickelson, who does have large hands, uses an interlocking finger grip with tremendous success. Other players have found they need to grip the club in what might be considered an unorthodox fashion in order to swing the club most effectively. Henry Picard, Masters Champion of 1937 and PGA Champion of 1938, injured his left thumb just before he played in the Masters of 1937. He decided to move his left thumb outside of his grip to lessen the pressure on it. The grip worked so well that Henry won the Masters and ever afterward used the same grip. That same grip was the immortal Gene Sarazen's for a lifetime.

Players who have short fingers sometimes feel that the amount of overlap afforded them in the Vardon grip is not sufficient to unitize the hands and thus prefer an interlocking style like Nicklaus's to achieve that meld. This is a very compact grip, and after the overlapping Vardon grip it may be the next most common grip in general use among golfers of the world.

The 10-fingered or modified baseball grip is just what the name implies: a grip with all the fingers plus the two thumbs used on the grip. There is no interconnection between the hands as in the Vardon grip. Those who have very small hands, or who seek more leverage rather than centrifugal force, find that the baseball grip with their levering style offers them greater speed and is more satisfactory than any other.

Here is an experiment I would like you to try. It will illustrate the necessity for the two hands to work together as a unit in the golf swing. Take a club in your hands and grip it with a two-inch separation between the top hand (your left, if you play right-handed) and your right or bottom hand. Try to swing at an imaginary ball with that grip. Notice how the right hand suddenly overpowers the left as it nears the bottom of the swing. This is a

The most common "neu-
tral" grip. The "V"s of the
right and left hands point
between the chin and right
shoulder. The left hand
shows two knuckles.

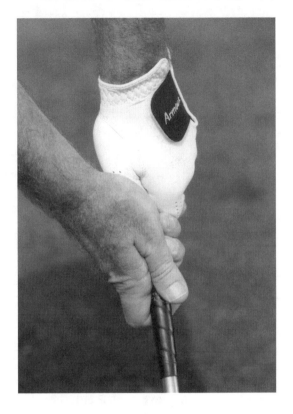

leverage action. Now, for a second experiment, slide your two
hands as close together on the shaft as you are able. Try another
swing. You will see that the hands are closer to working as a unit
rather than separately. This style utilizes more centrifugal force.

What we are seeking in the effective golf grip is a pair of hands
opposed to each other on the golf shaft but opposed to each other
in such a way that neither hand overpowers the other. You want
your two hands to work together as a unit. You want a compact
grip, not one in which one or the other of your hands is working
separately. Usually, one side of a person's body is more developed
and thus stronger than the other. The right-handed person usually
has a stronger right hand than left (the reverse is true for the natural left-hander). Because the right hand wants to deliver a strong
blow at the ball, it is necessary for the left hand, left wrist, and left
side of the body to be strong enough not to let the right hand take

control and overpower the left either before or at the moment of impact. In this book you will find my suggestions for exercises that will attempt to balance the right and left side power.

It is most important that you find the grip style that gives you *unity of hands*, one where there is no separation of the hands during the swing, no letting go, and where there is a balance of power. When you have settled on the right grip for you, you are well on your way to building a powerful golf swing.

Let's discuss the position of the fingers in a good golf grip. Some of the fingers are of greater importance than others in the grip. These are the last three fingers of the left hand and the third and fourth fingers of the right hand. There is also an important trigger point in the pad of the right forefinger.

The club must be held in the left hand so that it lies across the fingers at the bottom on the left hand (the first and second fingers) and then rides upward across the hand, eventually to be held

The club's grip runs across the base of the last two fingers of the left hand, where you can most effectively trap it against the fleshy pad of that hand.

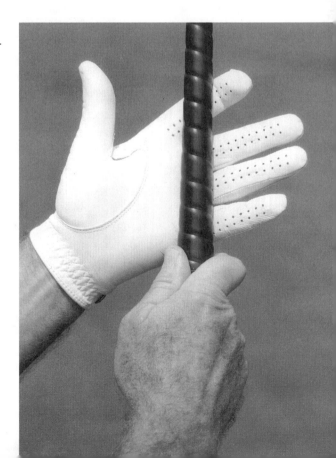

The club is basically controlled by a solid grip in the last three fingers of the left or top hand.

firmly against the pad of the left hand. It is of the utmost importance that the golfer build as much strength as possible in the last three fingers of his left hand. The left hand and those last three fingers are the primary controllers of the clubface position, thus influencing the degree of accuracy you have to accompany your length. The hands and fingers must be strong enough to withstand the considerable impact of the clubhead as it strikes the ball or turf. Since the ball is often struck at a point off center from the clubface, a strong twisting effect results, a torque that attempts to force the clubhead to turn. In addition, it has been demonstrated with individuals who have been electronically timed that those with more strength and mass to resist the torque effect of the club for off-center hits at impact drive farther and straighter than those with equal clubhead speed but less resistance. With a strong left hand and fingers, the golfer can reduce the torque and rebound and keep the clubhead on line through impact and follow-through. So in Chapter 3, you'll see specific attention paid to forearm and finger development.

Where the little finger of the right hand may be used to unify the grip by overlapping or interlocking, the other three fingers of the right hand are of great importance too. The club shaft lies more in the fingers of the right hand than it does in the left. Here is why. Gripping the club into the palm of the right hand tends to allow too much grip pressure and freezes the wrist from hinging at the top of the swing. It is this hinging action that provides you with additional potential power for clubhead speed. It's easy to visualize this. Extend your right hand out in front of you as though you were shaking hands. Now swing your arm back as though you were going to slap someone or something, but tighten your forearm so your right wrist won't hinge. Imagine the slap . . . or better, have someone extend a hand from the other direction so you can actually slap it. Now try again, but this time relax the muscles in your forearm and let your wrist hinge as your arm swings back. Repeat the slap. As you'll see, it will be with greater force. When you grip the club more in the fingers of the right

A right grip deep in the palm hinders the release of stored energy.

A finger grip in the right hand relaxes the tendons and ligaments across the wrist joint.

hand, it will allow you to get this setting or cocking movement in your hand and wrist.

Like so many things in golf, the feeling you get from this kind of grip is the opposite of what you'd expect. It feels weak but is actually strong because it will more easily allow the release of clubhead speed.

Placing the grip in the fingers of the right hand causes the club to lie between the first and second joints of the index finger. The fleshy pad just above the second joint is an important pressure point applied against the shaft and is another reason why the right-hand finger grip is crucial.

In the Vardon grip the little finger of the right hand overlaps the left index finger, either riding on top of it or else by sliding down into the slot between the first and second fingers of the left hand. (See photo on page 19.) Today, some form of the Vardon overlapping grip is used by 90 to 95 percent of the low-handicap golfers of the world.

The standard Vardon overlapping grip

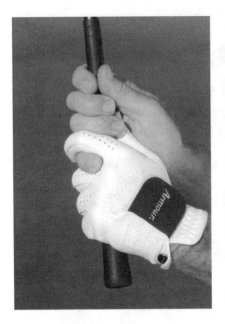

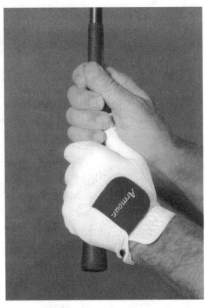

The interlocking grip laces the little finger of the right hand and the index finger of the left hand. But don't allow this connection to put the club's grip too deeply into the right hand.

The modified baseball or 10-finger grip should keep the two hands close together.

There are other options to the overlapping grip. The two most common are the interlocking grip and the modified baseball grip (sometimes referred to as the 10-finger grip). Each is pictured here. The basic principles we've discussed for the overlapping grip apply to these two options as well.

I suggest that you experiment with each grip to see if there is a difference. In my case, I grip the club using the overlapping grip with my little finger sliding down into the slot between the forefinger and the third finger of my left hand. Great golfers have gripped the club that way since Vardon first did at the turn of the century. Bobby Jones and Ben Hogan used the Vardon grip. So do Tom Watson, Arnold Palmer, Johnny Miller, Nick Faldo, and thousands of other golfers, many of whom have names you'd recognize.

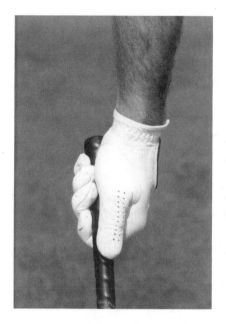 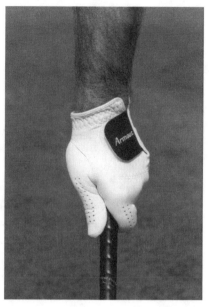

| This left-hand position with the thumb straight down the shaft and only one knuckle showing encourages a slice or fade. | The left-hand grip with the thumb on the side and three knuckles showing encourages a draw or hook. |

The rotational positioning of the hands is critical to the face position at impact. For example, the left-hand position can, by its location, encourage either a slice or hook.

PROPER AIM AND SETUP

What are we trying to do when we make a golf swing? The answer, of course, is that we are trying to drive a golf ball from *here*, a spot on the ground in front of us, to *there*, a definite target—the center of the fairway on a long hole, the green on a par-three hole, the flagstick, and the hole itself as we near the green.

On every shot in golf, the golfer is aiming or should be aiming at a target. The golfer must have a target in mind, a spot on the fairway or green, a distant tree or cloud where he can see "in his mind's eye" the ball's flight. As the late Harvey Penick said, "Take dead aim."

Accurate hitting of the target in golf requires a swing that consistently delivers the clubface square to the line toward the target. The best way to achieve that "squareness to the line" is to swing the club by approaching the ball from inside the target line. The golfer may even have the feeling that he is hitting from inside the line to the outside.

In a correct inside swing, you should imagine that you are part of a large wheel that rotates first to the right in your backswing and then to the left in your downswing. The club moves around your body like a spoke of that wheel with the clubhead traveling on the outer rim of the wheel. In order to achieve this wheel-like body motion, the arms remain close to the right side of the body.

The rotating motion around a swing center

It is obvious, too, that the center of that wheel moves very little to the right or left, up or down. In other words, the axis of that swing must remain relatively steady, in a turning motion that allows the body, arms, and hands to make a swing that will return the club-face to the place from which it started in the backswing.

The way you address the ball is most important because it involves physical comfort, correct aiming, and relaxation of tension. Each golfer should observe the same aiming routine every time he or she makes a shot. Walk up from behind the ball on the line to the target line for a moment, then with that line clearly in mind, step into the address position.

Stand to the ball so that it is directly between your feet, and then widen your feet about the width of your shoulders. Take your grip and allow your arms to hang straight down so that, from the front, you are in a perfectly "square-to-the-line"

This is good ball position
for a middle iron shot.

Bend at the hips, knees slightly flexed and arms hanging, for comfort and relaxed clubhead speed.

position as far as your head, shoulders, arms, legs, and feet are concerned.

Now, bend at the hips until your club touches the ground. The amount of bend will be greatest with the short iron clubs, such as

Here John Davis is shown standing too close to the ball, which inhibits power by restricting the release.

a wedge. Your knees should be slightly bent and relaxed and your tailbone should stick out a bit as though you were starting to sit down. The head is not dropped but should be kept level with the spine so as not to restrict your turn.

In an attempt to get more power, a golfer will often stand too far away from the ball. The result is frequently a loss of power, as the tendency is to hit the ball with the arms independent of the body.

Every golfer has to find his own proper address position. We all vary in our physical makeup. Some of us have longer arms than others; some people are long-waisted and short-legged. Others are just the reverse, short-waisted and long-legged. Each one of these physical attributes will affect the final combination of hands, arms, legs, and body in the golf swing setup.

In the beginning, you should position the ball on a line that runs at a true right angle to the target line within a range from about three inches inside of your left heel for a teed drive to a position with the ball in the center in line with your sternum for a short iron. Probably 80 percent of all golfers use this line and ball position with success, since it allows the clubhead to reach maximum acceleration just before it strikes the ball while still on the proper angle of approach. Furthermore, most golfers seem to feel more comfortable with the ball placed in this range.

However, a small percentage of golfers find their best success with the ball positioned more forward, while less flexible people with less lateral body movement toward the target may have it placed farther back. Don't be locked into a set ball position. Try various positions until you come to your own conclusion on the ball locations that allow you to hit the ball harder, straighter, and more consistently. Then keep those locations.

Be aware that as you place the ball more forward in your stance, you increase the difficulty of keeping your leading arm and clubshaft in a straight line at impact, as the wrist will tend to break down. It will also become more difficult for you to keep the clubhead moving down that line as it strikes the ball.

The reverse may be true as you experiment with moving the ball backward in your stance, more toward your right foot. You will find that it will become harder for you to get your clubface back to square with the ball as it strikes it. Unless you close the clubface more, your shots may start going to the right. Or, you may unconsciously attempt to force the clubface back to square and end up smothering the shot or hooking the ball badly to the left.

I suggest that you experiment to find your best ball position at address. Try the conventional spots first, and work out your swing from there.

My best advice to you and to all golfers is to trust your professional teacher to analyze your swing and help you find not only the best position of the ball at address but also every other "best position" for you in the grip, stance, at the top of your backswing, and in the other fundamentals of the swing.

Aligning the body to aim too far to the right, as Faye Bates is doing here, makes one either hook or come over the flight line and pull.

Square alignment of hips, shoulders, and arms parallel to the target line will help produce a proper swing path.

THE UNHURRIED BACKSWING

It is helpful to start your backswing leisurely. In my teaching career I have seen far fewer pupils who swung back too slowly than who swung back too fast. Excessive speed in the backswing seldom allows you to get to a solid position from which to return your swing. Fast backswings tend to be too short and may not allow for a weight transfer to the right leg. The rush in the backswing is made in an attempt to get speed in the hitting area. When the backswing length is too short to build momentum on the forward swing, then there is a flurry of activity, hurrying back in order to get through to the finish.

Trying to keep the head still over the ball in the backswing frequently results in a reverse weight shift (upper body hanging to the left side) at the top of the swing and a substantial loss of power.

When Jack Nicklaus needed to drive the par-four 18th hole at St. Andrews in the 1970 British Open, he said that he kept telling himself before he made the shot to swing slowly, "swing slowly." Well, he did drive the green, and that shot helped him to win.

The clubhead best starts back on a line roughly parallel to the golfer's shoulder alignment. If the club is snatched away in a quick, hurried movement, the relationship is destroyed at once and usually cannot be recaptured by any other compensating move. When a golfer swings back too quickly, snatching the club away from the ball, he chokes off his arm swing and body turn. It is important that you be in control of the club, not it in control of you. It's a backswing, not a back lift, back push, or back jerk.

If the width of the arc is lost at the top of the swing by snatching it up, it is difficult to recapture that important width coming down.

Those things happen when the club is taken away in too rapid a backswing. When the club is jerked away at the beginning of the swing, it almost inevitably follows that it will be rushed on the downswing as well.

It *is* possible to start your backswing too slowly. Too slow a takeaway also causes you to rush the forward swing in an attempt to generate clubhead speed. But I would rather see you swinging back leisurely, almost deliberately, for a while until you have impressed upon your mind the necessity of a swinging motion away from the ball, attempting to get a full windup and stretch. Then find the proper tempo that fits your swing and personality.

At the same time that I am urging you to swing back in an unhurried manner, I recommend that you start forward the same way. When I am driving my best, I have the feeling of getting set in a good position at the top of my swing and then starting down casually with the arms and hands while seeking rapid acceleration with the hips and trunk. The acceleration builds rapidly, but the start down is not hurried.

RHYTHM AND BALANCE

The word *rhythm* comes to us from ancient Greek and originally meant "music." It denotes a regularly patterned flow when used to describe physical activities. Maybe that's why some of our early great golf teachers used music in their lessons. The legendary Ernest Jones always used music and produced good player after good player. I myself have used music in golf schools and in my own game to enable rhythm and free-flowing movement. When we say that the golf swing should be rhythmical, we mean that each swing should have a regular flow from the moment the golfer steps into his or her stance and the golf swing begins until the golf ball is sent on its way and the swing comes to its natural conclusion. This is the critical link action chain of events that produces power. The term *rhythmical* applies to the consistent repetition of the same coordinated, measured golf swing time after time in an identical pattern, swing after swing.

A balanced finish is the result of a solid swing without tension. Good rhythm will help produce this position.

This rhythmical swing is best seen in the swings of the great golfers of our time. One of the finest examples of a repeating rhythmical golf swing was that of Sam Snead, winner of more PGA events than anyone in history. Whether he was hitting a full drive, a medium iron, or a short pitch shot, Snead always exhibited the same smooth, almost leisurely tempo in his swing. But the results he got with his smooth swing paid off in a consistently high acceleration of clubhead speed and beautiful golf shots, long and accurate.

The golfer's body in most swing styles moves from left to right and back to the left again in rhythmic sequence as he or she "feels" the proper balance from the soles of the feet up through the whole body. As this feeling of balance and rhythm pervades the entire body, the initial movement in the swing may come with a *forward* press, of hands and right knee to the left, a sort of kickoff that starts the club and the body into a reactive motion in a smooth takeaway from the ball in the other direction. For most players the forward press is a completely unconscious maneuver, an instinctive one that does not require any particular attention of the mind.

The next time you watch the stars of golf in action, pay particular attention to the various individuals to see if they use a forward press and how they do it. Gary Player's is particularly noticeable, as he *kicks* his right knee in toward the ball. Jack Nicklaus's forward press is less obvious: a firming of his grip as he starts the club back and a rotation of his head to the right at the same time. Then there is Phil Mickelson's, a more classic push forward of the hands before the backswing.

Not all good players use a forward press, nor do they all follow a left-right-left pattern with their weight. Some set up their upper body more to the right, particularly on a tee shot, and then simply wind over the right leg and shift back to the left. The choice of style can be likened to a baseball pitcher's. Some throw from a stretch with no one on base; others use a windup. Are they seeking velocity, accuracy, or a blend of the two? That's the same question you have to answer.

Whichever setup you choose (weight favoring the left, balanced, or favoring the right), I recommend that you practice swinging to a rhythm count or beat. You can count to yourself as you swing, like—"one, and two!" *One* is your backswing; *and* is your top and change of direction; *two* your forward motion. Music can help. Cassette recorders make music very accessible, and you should choose the style that best encourages good golf rhythm.

You must perfect your rhythm in order to consistently drive the golf ball a long way. It should be the same rhythm, swing after swing, for as we have discussed, any interruption of that rhythm means a likely breakdown in the link action and a subsequent loss of clubhead speed.

Your ultimate success at long driving depends upon many different factors: increased flexibility, which will give you a wider, longer arc; a sound platform or lower-body leg strength from which to "launch your projectile"; the speeding clubhead aided by a strong rotating torso; a solid square position at the top of the

John is using a wedge under his right foot to brace his leg so as not to sway to the right during the backswing. This will help his balance.

backswing so returning to the ball requires no adjustments; and more. But good rhythm that promotes *balance* and helps produce a proper sequencing of the swing is a foundation upon which to build.

Balance comes from proper setup, sound footwork, and swinging "within yourself," that is, at a pace your body can handle. How often have we seen inexperienced players swing much too hard at the ball and fall off balance? Believe me, balance at the finish of the swing is a great measuring tool for the swing's effectiveness.

I recommend that you watch the good players as they swing in balance. Pay particular attention to the way the left knee and left foot work inward to the right on the backswing and to how the right knee and right foot move forward to the left during the downswing. This is caused by proper hip rotation. Try to absorb and imitate the tempo of one of the players whose game you especially admire. The tall player should observe his counterpart on the PGA Tour, a player like Nick Faldo, Davis Love III, Tom Lehman, or Ernie Els. The shorter player should study Nick Price, Corey Pavin, Tom Kite, or Jeff Sluman.

I would like to call your attention to a teaching aid called *Fundamentals of a Model Swing.** It is a CD-ROM that features the graceful and balanced composite swings of PGA Tour players. On this disc, model swings are shown over and over again from several viewpoints with different clubs. The rhythm and balance of these swings are magnificent, helping you also to appreciate the acceleration and release in the swing. By studying these swings and watching these animations regularly, the mind becomes kinesthetically attuned to the rhythm and technique. It becomes clear in your mind how the swing operates. Confusion is swept away and your confidence builds, just as when you watch a golf tournament. Seeing these fine swings makes the striking of a ball seem much easier. This clarification in your mind and confidence that accompanies it will allow you to freewheel—and with that to get your best distance. I strongly recommend the concept of viewing such swing modeling programs.

---

*Available from Golf Around the World, The Learning Aids Company, (800) 824-4279

This is a closed-face position at the top. Note the arched wrist, the right elbow pointing down, and the face of the club to the sky, all of which encourage a hook.

Here is an open-face position at the top. Note the "flying" right elbow, opening of the left-hand grip, and toe of the club pointing down, all encouraging a slice.

Here is a square-face position at the top. The natural return from this position encourages a straight shot and the confidence to make a powerful swing.

THE SEQUENCE OF MOTION

The reversal of the direction at the top of the backswing down toward the ball is called the *transition move*. It is in my opinion the toughest move in golf. If it is done in proper fashion, the other motions in the golf swing flow in beautiful rhythmic sequence. It is the link action system from feet to legs through the trunk, back, shoulders, arms, and hands, all firing in proper sequence, that provides the maximum mechanical efficiency and the rhythmic flowing appearance. Under these circumstances you create a summation of forces that provides you with your greatest clubhead speed. The preferences and styles in golf swings will most certainly change in the years ahead, but the order in which the link system works is enduring. You can't improve on an absolute. When this happens correctly, the clubhead accelerates to its greatest speed just as it reaches the impact area.

The hips and pelvis should turn so the weight is over the right leg, which is the primary pivot point in the backswing.

It is most important that you understand the trigger point in your swing that starts your clubhead on its way back down to the ball. Your backswing in its windup or rotation has moved a good portion of your weight over your rear foot. You have wound up the muscles over the pivot point of your right leg.

Now—begin to unwind this bundle of energy by firing one link at a time. Start by moving laterally toward the target while rotating or uncoiling your hips. This will let you get your left heel back on the ground. If you have done it correctly, your left knee will separate farther from your right knee, which remains almost motionless in this first move in the downswing. Resist any temptation to begin to hit the ball with your right hand and arm. I assure you that your right hand and right arm "hit" will be there as it nears impact if you will obey this rule: *start your downswing with a left-side uncoiling move toward the target.*

Here is a strong windup with the upper body over the right leg and the lower body resisting to create more torque. Note the flexed right knee and back turned totally to the target.

The shift toward the target and unwinding have begun. The left knee has moved toward the target while the right has kept its position. The hands have maintained their cocked position.

The moment of truth—impact. While the weight is leaving the right side, the left arm is extended and in line with the shaft, the back of the left wrist is flat, the shaft angle is tilted toward the target, and the center of the body is slightly behind the ball.

As this lateral-rotary weight shift begins, accompanied by a pull down and a forward thrust with your left arm and left side, you will find that those muscles of your body so carefully coiled in the backswing are suddenly sprung loose, freed, and ready to help accelerate the golf club and clubhead along the return path to and through the ball at the impact area. You'll have that free-wheeling, slinging feeling.

I do not like the use of the term *hitting zone*, because I believe that term connotes a feeling of a forced-effort hitting swing rather than the idea of a flow that produces a swinging hit. The swinging hit is when the ball merely *happens* to be in the way of the club. I believe the golfer should imagine swinging the clubhead through a hologram, as if it's only an image. He or she will find no resistance whatsoever at the bottom of the swing, that the golf ball will be sent on its path almost by the accident of it being there.

This happens most effectively when the player projects his or her swing thought past the ball down the target line a few feet in front of the ball. It's a martial arts principle. If, for example, you are trying to break a board, you must not focus your attention on the board because that will produce tension just before impact, slowing your arm and hand speed. So the martial arts specialist always focuses on a point beyond the board and simply lets the board get in the way of his blow directed to that spot.

The practice of professional players using a spot on the ground in front of the ball as an intermediary target is effective not only for direction but also for distance. It's obvious that trying to swing toward that spot can help you establish a correct swing path. But have you ever considered that it also can free you from hit-instinct tension because your focus is past the ball?

MENTAL CUES

Let me suggest two mental pictures you can use to train yourself to perform this left-sided maneuver that begins the downswing. The thought I prefer, because it has worked effectively for me for many years, is that I am pulling my left arm forward so that my right elbow will drop toward my pocket. This "keeps the gun loaded" and stores your hit until the time when you can get the most speed from it. I find that the rest of my body obeys this command with the necessary counterclockwise rotation of my lower body and weight transfer, which in turn brings the clubhead to the ball with considerable acceleration. The other thought is to look down the range or fairway at your target with the feeling that you are going to unwind and sling the club right over your target, much like a hammer or discus thrower would unwind and let it go.

Experiment with both of these trigger thoughts to see if one works for you. Remember that your mind can hold only one thought at a time. The "right elbow to pocket" thought and the sensation of slinging are both single, positive thoughts. If you will concentrate on using either one in your game, you may discover that you have been able to block out of your mind any thought of hit or mishit and be able to freewheel.

A very important benefit that flows from the left-side pulling theory is that it plays down the premature-hit instinct of the right side in the swing. This is the most useful because, since most of us are right-handed, we instinctively want to apply our right-sided power to the swing. There is nothing wrong with a right-hand dominant leverage-type swing except that it frequently adds the right-side power too soon or in such a manner that the left hand is unable to withstand the force of the right-hand hit and collapses at impact. The result is often a mishit golf shot, a dreadful slice, or an awful hook.

IDENTIFYING A PROBLEM

All-time great Byron Nelson was once giving a clinic. After hitting a bad hook he commented, "Too much right hand." That shot was followed by a slice and Byron's comment again was, "Too much right hand." One spectator couldn't understand, so Byron explained. "On the first shot I hit with too much right hand too early, letting my left wrist break down, which closed the face and

Starting the forward swing with the hands too early causes a premature throw-away of stored power that comes from keeping the wrists cocked.

At the moment the clubshaft and the left arm form a straight line, the greatest speed is reached. Here the club has already passed that moment and deceleration has begun.

"Hitting from the top," or releasing your wrist-cock angle too early, will often result in the weight staying at the back foot and the swing path going left.

hooked the shot. The very next shot I used too much right hand, but this time I used it to squeeze and hold the rotation, leaving the clubface open and producing a slice. But both were too much right hand." That's not to say we can't use the right for power, but that most people need to emphasize the left so that the right does not totally dominate.

The most common fault on the downswing is opening the angle between your left forearm and the shaft too early—in golfer's lingo, "hitting from the top." The club in this move is thrown out and away instead of being held back inside the flight line by the cocked wrists. It is also important when making a "swinging hit" that you feel the weight of the clubhead speed to and through the ball. This creates an outward pull—centrifugal force, which operates most effectively when your grip pressure is not too tight and you have maintained your wrist cock well into the forward swing.

Golf's most critical move is the transition from the top of the backswing to the forward swing. It should be initiated by the lower body and should set the shaft angle in the correct plane.

Note that the shaft line is approaching slightly from the inside and would be parallel to the club on the ground if the hands were allowed to be hanging directly
in front of the body. The clubhead path will follow the direction the butt of the
club is pointing when in the in-front position.

Not "staying behind the ball" is a common golf swing mistake. It is equivalent to "coming off the ball." Both actions produce power loss and directional loss. In each case, the center of the swing has moved: in the first example, it has moved rearward away from the ball; in the second example, it has moved up and backward away from the ball. Although the true rotational center is at a point just at the top of the spine between the right and left shoulder, the player's head can be used as a functional reference point. The head remains level as the arms and club swing through. Many golfers are so anxious to see what has happened to their shots that they lift their heads much too quickly and spoil the result. You should keep your head relatively stable until it turns as a result of the right shoulder coming through to bring it up naturally. But be careful—keeping your eye on the ball or keeping your head down longer than after the natural release occurs will destroy sound footwork, good body action, and a complete finish. Don't ever look at the ground at the finish of your follow-through. Look at the target down the fairway.

Some teachers will claim that what you do after you strike the ball has no influence on the result. Technically, they are correct, but realistically, the practice of finishing your swing in good balance lends a great assist to what happens at the moment of impact. I recommend it especially for adding distance, because a follow-through that finishes short of a full finish is generally the result of slowing down somewhere earlier in the downswing. Likewise, the follow-through that finishes off-balance has been caused by a swing center that has moved too far, a faulty swing plane, or a mistimed application of power. With a good, accelerating swing the finish should be natural and uninhibited.

THE RELEASE

Another extremely important element in the power golf swing is that of release. What does *release* mean? Webster's dictionary tells us it means "to set free, to let go." Though Webster didn't teach golf, his definition applies. How many times have we hit a golf shot and left it short and right by "holding on," when we should have "let 'er go," or made a proper release?

Before we consider how a golfer achieves proper release in his or her golf swing, I would like you to picture some other action sports. These are a few ideas that will help you understand the feeling of release that you should have in your golf swing.

First, I would like you to visualize, in your mind's eye, an Olympic champion discus thrower. See the whole scene, the tremendous crowd in the stadium with all eyes focused on a magnificent athlete as he begins his throw. His right hand is cupped around the outer edge of the four-and-one-half-pound disc. He starts from a stationary position and begins to wind his body clockwise (the backswing) with his arm extended, holding the disc. He then whirls rapidly counterclockwise (the forward swing), and then at the precise moment he hurls the metal plate as far as he can.

I want you to imagine yourself flinging the discus. Wind, unwind, then feel the freedom of the release as the imaginary disc leaves your hand. Feel the acceleration that your body has built up before you let the plate go. Then, finally, feel the full extension, the releasing rather than tightening.

If you cannot picture yourself as a discus thrower, then try the mental picture of using a slingshot. Hold an imaginary "Y" out in front of you at arm's length and draw back the rubber sling. Put an imaginary golf ball in the sling. Now that the slingshot is at full extension, open your fingers and let it go. Again, you have a fine example of release, the sort of release you must have in your power golf swing.

Relevant to these imaginary games of release is a training trick a tennis coach used in teaching junior tennis stars. The coach would take about 20 old tennis rackets and put the student at the baseline of the court. Then she would order the student to throw the rackets overhand as far as he or she could. Eventually, the student was able to throw some of them into the backcourt. The result of this odd exercise was that the student learned to sense the

Players who squeeze the club too tightly would benefit from the feeling of winding up and throwing the club to get a better feeling of release.

proper release in the serve. The release training carried over when the racket was kept in the hand while making the serve.

The result of release in a golf swing is allowing the forearms to roll over 180 degrees while keeping their same basic relationship to the body as it turns through. Your right hand will reach a "shaking hands" position on each side of your body.

In the earlier example we gave of a karate expert smashing a board, he performs this remarkable feat using his force of *ki* to move his hand and arm through the board to a point beyond that of first impact.

During the approach, the right hand should feel light, as if almost off the club, and the right elbow should point toward the right front pocket.

The right hand is shown here in the correct release position of shaking hands when the swing is 90 degrees past ball contact.

Using a learning aid that provides resistance, like the Power Swing Fan,* encourages positive acceleration through the ball.

---

*Available from Golf Around the World, The Learning Aids Company, (800) 824-4279

This important idea is one I would like you to consider adopting for greater distance. Let the golf ball be the karate expert's board. See your target as a spot somewhere beyond, even down the fairway 225 yards away. You are going to swing *through* the golf ball, not at it.

THE FOLLOW-THROUGH

The final state of the swing, the movement of the clubhead through the ball, happens so quickly that it is impossible for the human eye to follow it. How do we know whether the swing has been executed properly?

There are ways to tell. First, we know by the sound and flight of the ball whether or not it has been well struck. Did the ball leap off the face, find its trajectory quickly, and just seem to keep going? If the drive starts low and then continues to climb steeply, you've hit a *riser*. A riser looks good but doesn't really produce maximum distance. It's caused by steep clubhead descent, giving the ball backspin and subsequent lift. A shallower angle of approach to the back of the ball is more effective. We can also tell a great deal about distance by the sound of the shot as it comes off the face of the driver. There is an unmistakable crack to a well-struck drive. You know it, and so do your opponents. But one of the best ways to tell whether the swing has been a good one is by watching the position of the body in the follow-through. A good follow-through is always the product of a good swing. A bad swing will produce an unbalanced or incomplete follow-through.

Let's define *follow-through* as it is generally understood in golf instruction. It is the finished position of the hands, arms, and body that is caused by the momentum of the club after the ball has been struck. In a good swing from an inside to on-line path, the clubhead attempts to chase after the ball but cannot because the hands hang onto it. So, the clubhead goes up and around the golfer's body. In a truly full follow-through after a good shot, the club can often be seen all the way around behind the player's body.

Here's the picture of a full follow-through. The player's weight has shifted entirely to the left side of his body and is focused over the heel and ball area of the outside of the left foot. Only the inside edge or toe of the right foot remains on the ground. The hips have turned until they are facing the target. The left arm, extended until the *moment of truth* at the bottom of the arc, is now bent and has folded so that the left elbow points toward the ground. The right arm has then folded and is over the shoulder. The back of the left hand may be in line with the forearm in much the same relationship that the hand and forearm had at the top of the backswing, although many players let the left wrist cup a bit more as they relax at the finish.

If there are flaws in the swing, they will immediately show up in an awkward follow-through. A prematurely released swing

A strong finish or follow-through is the result of an aggressive but tension-free swing.

from the outside leaves the golfer with much of his weight still on the rear foot. The golfer's hands will be low and around his body. The rear knee is apt to be pointing straight out at the ball's original position instead of being well past it, as it should be in a good swing. We all can recognize a bad swing just as readily as we can recognize and admire a good swing. The trick is how to do it . . . that is, make the good swing.

One way is to think *finish.* I'll frequently have my pupils "start at the finish." In this drill, they make a relaxed swing to a good finish position. I may make some adjustments. They hold that position for 15 seconds, then swing the club to the top of the backswing and return with speed to the finish. This takes their minds off the ball and focuses their attention on a point well past the ball, helping them to maintain clubhead speed through the impact area. The result is more distance.

THE SQUARELY HIT BALL

In striving for distance off the tee, many golfers fail to realize how important it is to strike the ball squarely. As you will discover in the discussion on the mechanical driving machine, a golf ball struck only one-half inch off the center of the clubface may lose from 10 percent to as much as 15 percent of its distance.

It is apparent from watching players on the first tee that many golfers believe they can consistently swing with more effort than they should and still hit the ball squarely with good clubhead speed. Often they accomplish neither result. The ball does not go far and it doesn't go straight because they have swung too *hard,* that is, with too much physical effort. When the ordinary golfer tries to slug the ball, he usually produces any one of several actions that actually hinder the momentum of the clubhead and prevent it from reaching maximum acceleration at impact. Some of these faults are: *tightening of the grip,* with the result that the muscles of the forearm are also tightened and thus are not free to produce the maximum clubhead speed or a square clubface; *a fast backswing,* which tends to pick up the club with the arms and hands rather than winding the upper body, causing the left arm to bend excessively and making it difficult to return the center of the clubface to the ball. This results in an ineffectual off-center hit and too short a backswing, with an inadequate coiling of the upper body, thus losing the power of the large trunk and back muscles. This definite power loss is often the result of the player rushing to find power.

The golfer must not overcontrol the clubhead at any point in his swing. The result is one you've seen so often in fellow players. It looks like they are trying to shove or push the club toward the ball. Overcontrol comes from trying to *make a golf shot* rather than letting a golf swing happen and a shot be the result. Overcontrol comes from trying to guide the motion rather than freewheeling it.

You must realize that the clubface is large enough to allow for considerable error and still hit the ball. As you practice more and more on a repeating path, you will also come to realize that you are striking it more frequently on the "sweet spot" of the face. That gives you the most effective power.

When that happens, there will come a new realization that *square hitting* of the golf ball results from a swing that is free from tension and overcontrol. It is imperative that every golfer *swing within himself or herself*, that is, not attempt to produce any more power than the power that results from his or her basic, uninhibited, full-motion swing without any conscious extra effort to either overcontrol or force the clubhead.

A wonderful thing happens when you stop trying to slug the ball. Concentrating on merely making solid, center-of-the-face, freewheeling contact with a rhythmical swing will actually add distance to your shots. You will hit the ball squarely more often than before, and thus you will get more force delivered to the ball consistently on more of your shots. This was well demonstrated to me personally on my record 381-yard drive effort of a few years ago. That shot happened to be the very first one of the competition, my first of six balls. After being announced, I approached the ball and said to myself, "Now, just swing it freely, hit it solidly,

An off-center hit such as on the toe . . .

. . . or heel causes considerable loss in distance.

Center face hits are the answer and can be tested with impact decals.

and get it inside the boundaries as a measurable shot. Then you can go after one harder." Well, the easy swing went 381 yards, and on the next five hard swings by trying to "hit it" 400 yards I snap-hooked it once, popped it up twice, and sliced it out-of-bounds

Good balance is essential in all sports. Proper footwork, as demonstrated here in the follow-through position, is the literal foundation of good balance.

twice. Don't try to slug the ball. Freewheeling full motion will produce less tension, get greater clubhead speed, and let you finish on balance. Maintaining balance is one of the greatest assets of the finest tour players' swings. How are they able to do that so consistently shot after shot? Because they swing within their controllable power limit rather than beyond it. They find an effective swing speed and don't try to exceed it.

When players do go for the "big tee ball," their approach is interesting. They generally slow down so they can get a bigger, longer turn and create more potential for distance. It has often been said that no golfer should exert any more than 90 percent of his potential power. I don't know if you can put an actual percentage on it, but you should feel that you have a little extra in reserve. It is difficult sometimes to do that. I know it is for me. But if you can keep some small feeling of reserve strength back, you will find that you are not only consistently longer and more accurate but that you have an additional psychological edge. You will feel confident, as if you're in control of your swing, not the swing in control of you.

"The most important muscles involved in the golf swing are those of the back, legs, forearms, and stomach (abdominals). Developing the muscles of the chest, frontal shoulders (anterior deltoids), and biceps can hinder the swing, actually making it more difficult to make a backswing."

DR. BILL MALLON, ORTHOPEDIST AND FORMER TOUR PLAYER

3
Training and Exercises

MY PERSONAL TRAINING PROGRAM

How fit do you have to be to play golf well? More so than you'd think. Physical deterioration or general lack of conditioning is the number one factor that causes the adult handicap to go up. If your handicap was at one time lower than it is now and you are still playing as frequently as you did before, look to your body first for the answer. Loss of strength and flexibility will alter technique. When your hands and forearms lose strength or suppleness and your straight ball turns into a slice, you automatically start to make adjustments in your aim, grip, and swing path. What you should be doing is conditioning your body.

Most of the PGA Tour players are athletes with a high degree of strength and flexibility related to their sport. Even those few Senior Tour players who sport a portion of their midsection outside their trousers have strong arms, hands, and trunks with more than adequate flexibility. Far more Tour players are fit than not. Physical training for golf is recognized on the Tour as an important factor in maintaining playing ability. The potential gains for any player are relative to the present condition of the body. The Tour players are already reasonably fit because they walk the golf course every day and exercise by hitting many balls. The weekend golfer generally is less so. For the player in poor physical condition, particularly seniors and especially senior women, the improvement in performance as a result of training could be quite significant.

Let's be honest. No one person has developed, tested, and conclusively demonstrated that his or her system is the best for increasing distance in all physical types. Claims may be made to this effect, but the fact is that the same prescription does not work for everybody. For example, a senior player may have above-average strength but be badly lacking in flexibility. Conversely, a female player may possess extreme flexibility but be lacking in strength. Each needs a training program geared to his or her weak-

One of the predominant physical factors that differentiates men's and women's golf is strength. Here Faye, who plays a nice game but whose good drive may reach but 155 yards, cannot support the weight of two clubs held at arm's length. Added strength would make a difference.

John, who can drive 275, can hold three.

ness. Training to improve physical deficiencies as well as inadequacies in the swing will be an important part of the serious golfer's future.

I'd like to share some training thoughts based on my experience, observation, and experimentation. I certainly don't claim this is the only training program for everyone, but for my objectives of hitting the ball longer, developing better swing technique, and acquiring sufficient endurance to play on successive days in a tournament without undue fatigue, this program works.

Strength

What do I do for strength? First, I want reasonable total body balance with special emphasis on the fingers, hands, back, trunk, and legs. My primary strength-building system is based on progressive weight training using machines, although free weights and cable apparatus can also be used. The reason I've chosen machines is that they allow me to isolate specific muscle groups, and the equipment is comfortable and relatively safe. There may be better training regimes for golf, but machines that isolate and provide resistance are so widely accepted and distributed that the equipment is readily accessible for most people in their communities. I also use secondary strength developers such as "The Distance Builder" from Golf Around the World, a hand exercise gripper, and some calisthenics that I'll discuss later. If I dropped machines and used these secondary developers exclusively, I could still create a useful workout.

To develop strength you need overload. Overload makes your muscles do more work than that to which they are accustomed. You accomplish this by increasing either the load lifted or the number of times you lift the load. A simplistic example would be to load a leg-extension machine with the amount of weight you can lift 8 times consecutively. Do that on Monday, then 9 times on Wednesday, and 10 times on Friday. On the following Monday, add five pounds and go back to 8 repetitions. That's simple overload. The body needs the in-between days for resting and rebuilding the muscle tissue. Light daily workouts are possible and may be effective for the golfer, but the pros who work out vigorously need rest days. One workout per week for the trained athlete is not enough to maintain his fitness level. For the untrained—the person who does little or nothing—it will improve his condition up to a point. Two days a week can definitely improve your condition; three or four times a week is the most beneficial because your effort does not have to be terribly intense, and you still are giving the body a day off.

Intensity is something you must treat very carefully. While the greatest gains come from the greatest intensity, you need to be careful. This is not a weight lifting contest. Frankly, my biggest weakness is working out too hard before I'm adequately trained, causing either overfatigue or injury.

For golf I'd counsel to *train, don't strain*. If you are out of condition and it has taken you 20 years to get that way, don't try to reverse your condition in two weeks or you'll likely become an exercise dropout. Your anticipated feeling of dynamic health will turn into one of fatigue and soreness, the by-products of doing too much, too soon.

Exercising regularly is far more important than achieving big increases in the amount of weights you lift. On most weight stack machines, for example, the plates are loaded in 10-pound increments. For many of your golf exercises, increases should be undertaken in 5-pound increments. This can be accomplished by using loose plates, which are available at any fitness center.

When I'm not on the road, a workout week would look something like this:

Monday
Morning—stretching and routine exercises, 15 minutes.
Afternoon (either at lunchtime or after work)—workout on machines, sit-ups, and flexibility work. Total time: 30–40 minutes.*

Tuesday
Morning—jog and stretching; Distance Builder, Gym-in-a-Bag power pull, and sit-ups.

---

*My goal in the past year has been 100,000 sit-ups or crunches.

Wednesday
   Same as Monday.

Thursday
   Same as Tuesday.

Friday
   Same as Monday. Sometimes I skip Friday and do my machines at the fitness center on Saturday. If the fitness center is visited on Saturday, I run Sunday.

Saturday
   Same as Thursday, although my run is more often in the afternoon or evening, as I play golf Saturday morning.

Sunday
   Rest. Sometimes a short jog and sit-ups.

This workout schedule is light to moderate for an athlete in training but somewhat ambitious for the busy working person with a family who is trying to get in some golf time. However, it can be done if you eliminate some of your television watching and are willing to get up a little earlier in the day.

The Fitness Center Workout

Fitness center training has swept the country. Understand that there is no magic in any particular line of equipment; although some brands or systems are better than others, you should try different kinds of machines. They all are effective to various degrees in developing strength, maintaining flexibility, and, in some instances, aiding cardiovascular fitness. But *you* still have to produce the physical work.

Students are usually encouraged to perform the whole line of exercises to get muscular balance, with little attention paid to specificity of sport. I agree with that concept for general health and fitness, but I disagree if you want to swing a golf club effectively. A certain percentage of the population is so poorly conditioned that any exercise would help them, regardless of their sport. But in a finely tuned skill activity like golf, in which a certain pattern or sequence of motion is critical, it's different. That is why I'm advocating that the use of any weight-training system be limited to certain exercises, depending upon your needs.

There are some exercises to shun and others to do with guarded enthusiasm. If you feel that you are really out of shape, go ahead and do the regular program. But if you already have a modest level of fitness, I would consider the following recommendations:

1. *Biceps Curls*, even if practiced through a full range of motion, will tend to shorten your arc length in the golf swing. There is no move in golf that resembles the biceps curl, unless it is a counterproductive move. *Stay away from too much work on the Biceps Curl.*

2. *The Triceps Press* can have some value, particularly if the emphasis is on your left arm. The left tricep does play a role in pulling the arm toward the target, and both the right and left tricep play a role in arm extension. However, developing bulk in the triceps can inhibit the pattern of your arm swing across your chest. Do this exercise, but with caution, watching out that you don't build bulk.

3. *The Chest* or *Bench Press* is not a highly recommended exercise for golfers, since the larger the pectoral muscles in the chest become, the farther the arms must swing away from the body. Though the pectorals do contract in the golf swing as stabilizers, they contribute little to the force of the swing. If the pectorals are overly developed, they can definitely detract from the desired technique.

4. *The Military Press* or *Arm Press* is a deltoid (shoulder) developer, which enhances movements that are not of particular value to the golfer. In fact, you must be very careful not to inhibit the suppleness of the shoulder girdle and fluidity of the arm swing. Powerful deltoids pull the golfer's shoulders back: a classic position for the sculptured body

of a gymnast or bodybuilder, but detrimental to the golfer. Give me the round-shouldered athlete with muscles bulging in his or her back, not the upper front.

We've dwelled on the negative; what about the positive? What *should* you emphasize?

The machines that I use are listed in the order in which I use them:

1. *Back Extension*—Bad backs debilitate golfers at all levels of play; the golf swing does put stress on the lower back, which makes this machine a must for golf training. Caution: Work more for repetitions, not extremely heavy loads.

This is a back extension machine. The lower back is a critical part of the anatomy to strengthen for golfers to produce power and help prevent injury.

In making the extension, keep the upper body lines straight; return to the starting position more slowly than in the extension.

2. *Leg Extension*—This muscle group is a weakness of mine, since I had knee injuries from college football and then knee surgery five years ago. For that reason, I work hard on this exercise, although I don't rate it as high for golfers in general as several other exercises. The free-weight equivalent of this exercise is sitting on a table and extending your leg with a weighted boot on your foot.

3. *Leg Press*—Here is an important exercise for almost every sport, as it develops the large quadriceps muscles in the thighs (see photo below).

4. *Leg Curls*—This is basically a leg exercise for the hamstrings, but takes on added importance for golf because of its work on the buttocks and lower back.

5. *Lat Machine*—The latissimus dorsi muscles are the large muscles in the back that run from under the arm up to the level of the shoulders and across the back to the spine. They are contributors to the series of link actions

Leg presses develop the quadriceps, or thigh muscles, the largest in your legs.

that make up the golf swing. You needn't pull the bar behind your head to 100 percent flexion. For golf I'd recommend the 60 percent range.

6. *Cable Pulls*—Using a cable cross machine mimics a forward golf swing motion with first a left pull, then a right pull, then a pull with both hands. Use your trunk rotators and back muscles for the power. Make the angle of your pull low rather than steep (see photos below).

7. *Adductor-Abductor*—This is a good golf exercise for the inner and outer leg. It contributes to the player's ability to maintain balance and a solid foundation (see photo on page 70).

Cross cable exercises that mimic the golf swing positions approaching and through impact are some of the best power moves you can experience in the training center. Use both the left side . . .

. . . and the right. Work on the trunk rotation and back muscles with the arm more as a stabilizer. Do contras in the other direction for muscular balance.

The adductor-abductor machine works the inner and outer thigh muscles and helps in your balance and stability during the swing.

The abdominal or stomach muscles, another important muscle group for golf
power, are being worked here.

8. *Abdominal*—The muscles of the stomach are important for posture and for helping to prevent low back pain. The center of the body is also an important part of your power link system.

9. *Rotary Torso*—An exercise machine not found in many fitness centers, but one that is particularly good for the golfer. This machine strengthens and stretches the muscles that rotate the torso and that are so much a part of the golf swing (see photo below).

10. *Triceps Press*—You want strong (but not large) triceps. This machine helps develop the muscles to stabilize the left arm as it pulls in a horizontal extension and gives extension to both arms.

The rotary torso machine provides one of the best exercises for golf.

11. *Rise on Toes*—This is done most easily on a leg press machine by straightening your legs and pressing the weight by extending the foot (see photo below).
12. *Side Bends*—Do these on a cable machine, with a hand strap alternating between the right and left side.

Above all else, work on exercising your back, particularly the lower back. Bad backs have shortened more golf careers than any other injury. The muscles of the lower back are important in helping prevent poor posture, which leads to disc and nerve problems. The stress loads placed on the back in a vigorous, athletic golf swing are substantial. If you are in pain and can't use your back muscles properly, you have lost a powerful element in your link action system. More important, you probably can't practice or play.

The Distance Builder*

Players have been encouraged for years to swing a weighted club to develop stronger golf muscles. I've received reports from several

While on the leg press machine you can also do rises on toes for the calves, or gastrocnemius muscles.

*Available from Golf Around the World, The Learning Aids Company, (800) 824-4279

The Distance Builder incorporates progressive resistance exercises and can be a key to a home training program. To strengthen the forearms, rotate the Distance Builder or weighted club 180 degrees. Repeat 8 to 10 times, over and back, with each arm. Grip higher or lower to change resistance, or you may add more weight.

This exercise is called "over-the-shoulder wrist cocking." Keep the back of the left hand flat, cocking the wrists so the weight is lifted alternately over the left then right shoulder.

A triceps press exercise can be accomplished by holding the Distance Builder behind your back, elbow high in the air, and bringing the weight up to vertical while keeping your arm and weight in line with one another.

This exercise is "behind-the-back wrist cocking." Elevate the weight to the rear by cocking the wrist and keeping the weight and your arm in the same line.

Make a full swing with the weighted Distance Builder without losing good form. If the weight causes you to lose form, it is too heavy.

Follow through to a good release position on the other side of the body while maintaining good form, and complete the swing to a full finish.

players who say they have profited from this experience. However, not all biomechanics scholars would agree that it will increase your swing speed. In fact, some would contend that it interferes with technique.

My personal feeling is that this latter theory might be true at the highest levels of performance, during the professional season, but the benefits of strength and flexibility gained by the multitude of golfers who need those qualities far offset any interference with their technique. In fact, the added strength and flexibility would afford most of them an improved technique.

The Distance Builder is a golf-club-like apparatus that progressively adds resistance in the form of weighted rings. As the golfer grows stronger, he or she adds another ring. I swing it for three sets of 12 repetitions, with 30-second rest intervals between each set. Every other session, I add one ounce of weight. I try to swing my best full-driver swing—with as close to perfect form as possible—and I stop adding weights or, if necessary, take off weights whenever my form starts to deteriorate. After the three sets with the Distance Builder, I take a regular driver and swing for speed, emphasizing good form, a feeling of freewheeling, and an uninhibited swinging motion. And finally, I use a driver shaft with no clubhead to focus even more on speed of body movement. That comprises a power-swing workout session.

If you do not have weight training facilities of any kind readily available, using the Distance Builder alone can have a surprising benefit. There are also several exercises you can do besides simply swinging the Distance Builder. The series shown in the previous pictures includes pronation-supination, triceps-behind-the-back, over-the-shoulder wrist cocking, and behind-the-back wrist cocking.

Built-In Training at Home or Office

There never seems to be enough time to get everything done. Our good intentions so often fall short of fulfillment. We are always going to practice the piano, work on our German vocabulary, read the latest bestseller, run three miles, write those overdue letters, hit golf balls, and do our exercises. But the day passes and today's

After using a heavy object like the Distance Builder, take a raw shaft (no club-head) and swing it for speed.

Maintain good form while using a raw shaft. Always swing to a full finish. Listen for the speed.

If you don't have a raw
shaft, turn your driver
around so you are gripping
the neck, and create your
greatest speed.

goal becomes tomorrow's promise. Worse yet, "one of these days I'm going to" eventually becomes "none of these days," and the dreams of accomplishment fade as we realize the time is gone irrevocably. That doesn't have to happen if you learn to build in the practice time toward your goal as a habit each day in your life.

Several years ago, I did a feature in *Golf Digest* that I called "Bathroom Exercises." These are exercises that you can associate with some other habitual activity and build into your daily routine. For example, you can do sit-ups during television commercial breaks, or use a grip squeezer at your desk by the telephone or in the front seat of the car. The "bathroom exercises" are as follows:

BATHROOM EXERCISES

Daily Activity	Exercise Attached to Daily Activity
Turn on the shower water and let it get hot.	Back-scratch and side-bend stretching, fingers laced over head.
Turn on water for wash basin, let water get hot and basin fill up.	Lace fingers, raise arms overhead, and reach to the sky.
Wash and lather for shave or do makeup.	Repeated rise on toes.
Shave or do makeup and hair.	Isometric tummy and buttocks tightener. Hold for 30-second sets.
Brush teeth.	Two-legged, or one-legged, half-knee bends or squats.
Put on deodorant.	Achilles stretch, reach to ceiling one arm at a time.
Use aftershave, facial cream, or oil.	Raise leg and rest it extended on sink or chair. Bend forward, head toward knee, and stretch hamstring. Alternate legs.
Leave bathroom.	Pause in doorway and do isometric arm exercises or a turning wall touch.

Hand grippers like this sit on the ledge next to me in the car, by the TV in the family room, and next to my office phone. It is the single most important exercise a golfer can do for club control.

Back Scratch—with your
left hand reaching down
your back, grab your elbow
with the right hand and
push downward to increase
shoulder flexibility. Then
repeat with the other arm.

Side Bends—clasp your
fingers over your head and
bend to the side in line
with your body. Hold that
position for 10 to 15
seconds, then reverse
the direction.

Reach for the Sky—lace your fingertips together, palms pushing upward, and stretch to your greatest height by standing on your toes.

Toe Grab—using a bench or chair for support, elevate your leg and rest your heel on the seat. Keep your leg extended and gradually reach forward until you can hold your toe (or as close to that as you can get). Hold for 15 to 20 seconds and reverse legs.

Wall Touch—standing
about one foot away from
a wall and while keeping
your feet flat on the floor,
turn your upper body to
where you can touch the
wall with both hands. Hold
for 20 to 30 seconds and
then reverse the direction.

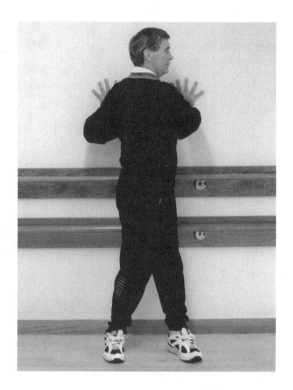

This is almost a personal daily ritual (no one is 100 percent). It's not much—but it is something. If I get shut out from the rest of my normal routine because of an impossible schedule, at least I've gotten in my bathroom exercises. Occasionally, I swim, which I think is productive in helping a golfer loosen and relax his or her body. Bicycling would be my first substitute for jogging, either stationary in front of the TV or actual riding in the neighborhood. Jogging is a part of my program, although I am only a casual jogger, going about four to eight miles per week. I'm not training to run. I'm training to finish a golf round without undue fatigue and to simply feel better for anything I do in life.

Built-ins are a blessing for the busy, motivated person. Think of some things you do every working day and attach a built-in activity to it. When you roll out of bed, how about rolling right onto the floor and doing those stretching exercises? Or, why not build in the bathroom exercises? If yours is normally the coffeepot and

TV routine, make the television-watching time productive. I've done sit-ups to the *Today* show on NBC for several years. The jog before breakfast—and for me before TV—is a Tuesday, Thursday, and weekend ritual. It's no big thing—a couple of miles each time—but it's regular. It raises my pulse to between 130 and 150 beats per minute, which is where I want it to be for cardiovascular improvement. Again, I'm training to finish strong on the 17th and 18th holes, not to compete in the latest marathon run in my neighborhood.

How do you get to work? Can you ride your bike? Can you walk? Either could have a fitness component built in. Like most people, I drive to work, but on the dashboard of my car is a grip squeezer. Forearm flexor-muscle exercises are built in as I simultaneously work on another part of my training—the mental part. Playing over the car speakers is a cassette tape, and I'm hearing some of the best speakers and motivators in the world. They are all available on audio cassette. The most complete selection of speakers to shape your attitude for positive, aggressive, winning golf comes from the Nightingale-Conant Corporation of Chicago. Although the subject may not be specifically golf, the pattern and formula for success is much the same in all activities. It centers around confidence, mental toughness, perseverance, a positive attitude, imaging success, and the ability to relax. So, built into my ride to the office is a short but regular practice period. Personally, I find this one of the greatest sources of built-in benefit, all because of the availability of a couple of simple strength tools and a free tape from my local library featuring some great people to listen to. On the other hand, that same drive to work could add up to a lot of wasted time. That's your choice.

The office where I used to work had an elevator. I seldom used it. I've watched too many people with nice figures get chained to a desk, take two coffee breaks and lunch each day, eat doughnuts and cake every time there is a birthday in the office, plus regularly ride the elevator. It takes about three years to see the spread set in, but it's inevitable and uncomplimentary. Climbing the stairs would at least help the legs. In golf, when you lose your legs you lose your platform, your base, your source of stability. Riding in elevators and golf carts won't help.

Office work is sedentary. It's tough to be an athlete, a golfing athlete, when the exercise in your job consists of lifting mortgages, running up quotas, balancing ledgers, pushing sales, or pulling some strings. I'm lucky. The closest workout facility, at PGA National, is only a few minutes away. When I worked in an office I seldom ate lunch away from the office. Most of the time it was a yogurt or a light sandwich at my desk. But on Monday, Wednesday, and Friday I took what time I'd spend on lunch away to get in a 30-minute workout on the exercise machines followed by a short, relaxing swim. Time away from desk: one hour. On the weekend, I focused more on my golf and running.

Priorities

If it's strictly golf improvement you are after and your free time is limited, I'd choose the following activities in order of their contribution to golf improvement for people who are in decent physical condition.

1. Take instruction, then practice, particularly on the short game.
2. Play golf, working on mental control and course management.
3. Practice swinging—doing drills, visualizing, and feeling the swing.
4. Do machine exercises or calisthenics related to golf strength and flexibility.
5. Jog, bicycle, swim, or do built-in exercises.

If your level of fitness is poor, then exercise has to move up on the priority list. (In fact, without it, the other activities may be a waste.) Doing all of these things is that much better. We have given considerable space to the development of strength. But you must understand that flexibility is more important for distance than people realize. The primary cause of decreased distance in men is the loss of the range of motion or flexibility, *not* loss of strength. Obviously, both take place as we age. However, restricted motion in men leads more to a poor technique than does decreased strength. And technique is still a critical factor in producing distance.

Therefore, I recommend that you include flexibility exercises, such as some of those contained in basic Hatha yoga, to keep your spine, back, shoulders, and trunk as flexible as possible. Those pictured previously are very useful for golf.

Developing a good golf swing will bring you as close to your potential distance as any single factor. Specialized training for strength and flexibility, having the right equipment, and having the right state of mind will all enhance your distance production, but in smaller increments. The only exceptions to that are people in such poor physical condition that for them swinging a golf club properly is out of the question until their body is fit enough to do it. That includes a lot of golfers.

Practicing the short game using a readily available alignment tool pays big scoring dividends.

Gary Wiren's Personal Training Program

Strength Exercises: three days per week

Fitness Center
(Exercises using a machine are indicated by an *.)
- Warm-up stretching
- Sit-ups on incline bench or curl-ups
- Cable pulls left and right*
- Side bends
- Back extension*
- Abdominal*
- Rotary torso*
- Leg extension*
- Leg press and calf press*
- Leg curl*
- Ad-ab*
- Triceps press*
- Lat machine*

Distance Builder
- Flat-wrist over-the-shoulder cocking
- Pronator-supinator, right and left—180 degrees
- Behind-back wrist cocking
- Triceps overhead extension
- Regular swing
- Swing for speed (light club or shaft)

Flexibility Exercises
- Salute to the sun—Hatha yoga
- Golf flexibility series, in between strength sets

Cardiovascular Exercises
- Jogging—two miles three times per week or three miles two times per week
- Swimming
- Bicycling

General Exercises
- Sit-ups or curl-ups, back extension
- Back extension on floor

Built-In Exercises
- Hand exercise gripper
- Bathroom exercises

On the Road
- Rubber tubing or rope for door jamb pulls
- Jogging or stair climbing
- Floor exercises

Leg Overs—while lying on a padded surface or mat, elevate one leg and while extended swing it slowly to the side until it touches the floor. Return to your starting position; then repeat with the other leg in the opposite direction. This is a great floor exercise for trunk flexibility.

Another training device for building stronger hands, wrists, and arms is RGT Wrist Builder, available from Golf Around the World, (800) 824-4279, used for flexion (reversed for extension).

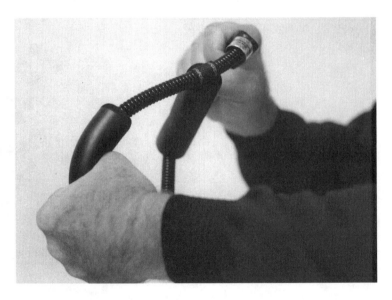

It may also be used for pronation and supination, an exercise seldom available in other pieces of equipment.

Hand and Arm Strength

In a test conducted on a mechanical ball-hitting machine, modifications were made to create a more human-like result. Instead of having the machine grip the club in its usual viselike fashion, the investigators were allowed to put sponge rubber around the grip, much like the fleshy pad of the hand. In addition, the pressure applied by the clamps was similar to that exerted by a human hand. The purpose of the test was to compare the results of off-center hits when gripped in the normal viselike fashion versus the more human, softer method. "Sweet spot" hits traveled relatively the same distance, but in the off-center hits, the softer grip produced far more dispersion and deviation from a straight path than the firmly clamped shots. Tight gripping by the player is not the answer; a firm yet relaxed grip is. Tightness doesn't work because it restricts the action in your forearms and wrist, producing a stiff-looking and slow-moving clubhead. You need strength in your arms and hands for firmness and to be able to accomplish it by gripping lightly, not tightly. If you are strong, you can control the club without exerting great tension in your hands and arms.

THE MIND AS WELL AS THE BODY

Does the mind really affect long driving, or is long driving strictly the domain of the physical and mechanical? You can easily answer that by attending any athletic event where the performer is attempting to produce a maximum physical effort, such as in weightlifting, shot-putting, the high jump, the long jump, the pole vault, or similar track events. In the moments before these sports performances, there is inevitably a great deal of self-psyching—using the mind to prepare the body for peak performance. The mind most certainly has an effect. It does in golf as well, but in a different manner. The production of power is not the only issue. Control and consistency must be blended with power. Instead of *psyching up*, in golf the mind is more frequently used to *psych down*, or to reduce the tension level. What you want is a high energy level and lower tension level, an almost cavalier Fred Couples, Fuzzy Zoeller, Lee Trevino, or Jesper Parnevik approach to the whole thing where you are enjoying the experience and free-wheeling. Tension is the great destroyer of a mechanically effective swing. So avoid tension—it's a distance killer.

Your body won't lie for your brain. If you are saying to your-self, "This one is going 260 right down the middle . . . 260 . . . 260 . . . ," and when you get to the top of your backswing an inner voice says, "Don't slice it out-of-bounds," you have no chance. Inevitably, you'll hit from the top and pull across the ball or tense your body so badly the arm and hand release will be *blocked out*, sending the ball in the very place you were trying to avoid. In any case you'll most certainly not get the kind of surprising distance that comes from a more relaxed, freewheeling state of mind. The license to freewheel is issued by the mind. And your mind must be broadcasting positive pictures.

I call it *surprising distance*, because you don't feel as though you are expending a great deal of physical effort. It almost feels like a full-motion practice swing. Let me give you an example. I had a student who could make a 2-handicap practice swing, but when the ball was put down in front of him, he barely played to his actual 18 handicap. The smooth-flowing, accelerating, sling-ing, uninhibited, whistling motion when his target was only air turned into a jerky, abbreviated, slashing, tension-filled lunge when the ball was placed in the way. Obviously, the problem was not physical or mechanical. This golfer had all the strength, flex-ibility, and technique that was needed to produce distance. Otherwise, he couldn't have made such a beautiful practice effort. What was keeping him from repeating that swing was the sight of the ball. We tried everything: "Pretend it's a soap bubble," "Hit it with your practice swing," "Swing through, not at," "Close your eyes," and the teacher's inevitable last-straw comment, "Just relax." The advice was to no avail. The pattern persisted: well-paced, fluid practice swings *through* to the target . . . followed by disaster—a muscularly tight, forced hit *at* the ball. One evening while at home my cerebral light went on. I had remembered reading of a plausible solution—a trick. The next day I bought a half-dozen hollow plastic balls, ones with solid exteriors, no holes in them, and I painted them black. I also got a half-dozen high-compression *real* balls and painted them black. I called my pupil. When he arrived I showed him the dozen balls, and with a statement of intended deception (much like a carnival sleight of hand expert) said, "Now we have here a dozen black plastic balls." I proceeded to demonstrate with a plastic example that they wouldn't bounce off the concrete any higher than my ankle and when struck full force would die at 30 yards. I told him, "Why try to hit hard . . . it won't go anywhere . . . just swing!"

I placed the first black plastic ball on the tee. He looked convinced. Apparently he was, because he put his practice swing motion on the first shot and sailed a beauty out there about 25 yards. Then another and another. "See how easy it is." On the fourth shot I slipped in one of the real balls painted black. It was next to impossible to tell the difference. He swung. You should have seen his face! The most beautiful, effortless drive—240 yards—straight as the state lines in Colorado. He had actually hit one with his practice swing. The mind, in this case, just needed to be tricked.

But developing a good golf mind is not just about tricks. The mind can also be trained. The training for hitting your longest tee shots requires that you see positive results in order to let you free-wheel. Pick an area where you want the ball to go—but not some target so precise it tightens you up. Visualize your swing and the flight of the ball, its trajectory and shape. Then rehearse your swing to reinforce freedom of motion and pace—and let it go. Let me caution you, however, about standing over the shot too long. If you are seeking precise accuracy, a little extra time in your shot routine might be helpful. But if it's your longest distance you are seeking, without having the narrow confines of a tight driving area, I'd suggest this little routine that I use for those long, wide-open par-fives. Simply incorporate these three words in your preshot routine: *Ready—Aim—Flier! Ready* is seeing your visual picture and placing both hands precisely on the grip; *Aim* is getting the clubface and body aimed where you desire; and *Flier* is winding up and letting the clubhead fly toward your target. These are simply thoughts and pictures of the mind, but they have a great deal to do with tension reduction and therefore with distance.

" . . . A golfer who learns to swing hard initially can usually acquire accuracy later, whereas a golfer who gets too accuracy conscious at the outset will rarely be able to make himself hit the ball hard later on."

JACK NICKLAUS

4
Equipment

A DRIVER THAT FITS YOUR GAME

Your driver is one of the most enticing clubs in your bag. If you have confidence in it, you can't wait to tee up that brand-new golf ball and give it a ride. On the other hand, for many golfers, the driver is an intimidating club. Memories of shots out-of-bounds, of topped or skied drives, cause many a golfer to fear his or her driver. Some golfers even reconcile themselves to the fact that they simply cannot handle the driver. They resort to using a three-wood or even an iron and get less distance off the tee. For a temporary cure this may be smart, but for the long run you are at a distance disadvantage if you can't use your driver.

Although it may take some searching and some experimenting, you can find a driver that fits your swing. Here are some important checkpoints for you to consider in choosing a suitable, effective driver, one that will help you drive the ball longer and straighter:

1. Shaft flex
2. Shaft length
3. Shaft material
4. Head and face material
5. Face angle (open, square, closed)
6. Face loft
7. Lie angle
8. Swing weight and overall weight
9. Depth of face
10. Face progression (degrees forward or back of shaft)
11. Aesthetics—do you like its looks?

One of the most critical elements in your driver is its shaft flex. Since it is the longest club in the bag, it tends to flex more than any other in the swing. In order to check whether you are using the proper shaft flex for you, you must analyze your present driving results. If you are hitting high hooks most of the time, it could be an indication that your shaft is too flexible for you. If you are hitting low shots to the right with a fade, it is probably a sign that the shaft is too stiff for you.

High-speed cameras show us that the lower end of the shaft bows forward and downward as it approaches impact. Picture the shaft at impact as a gentle curve to the left (for right-handers) from your hand to the ball. The more flex the shaft has, the more it will bend. For each half-inch that the lower end bows forward the clubhead will close approximately two degrees. Obviously, the stiffer shaft bows less than the more flexible shaft. That is why golfers who get high clubhead speed need stiffer shafts for control of the face and trajectory.

The conventional length of a man's driver used to be 43 inches, but today 44 inches to 45 inches is more common, with even longer lengths available. There is no question that the longer the club, the longer the swing arc. But, the longer the club, the farther the golfer is from the ball. And the farther away the golfer is from the ball, the more difficult it is for him to return the clubface to the same place every time and strike the ball on the center of the

The three drivers here range in length from 42 inches to 46 inches. The longer the club, the greater the potential leverage and speed, but the more difficult to control.

face. So again, you may have to trade off increased length in your driver for loss of accuracy and solid hitting. I recommend that only the low-to-middle-handicap player use a driver longer than 43 inches. Most golfers with higher handicaps do not have grooved swings, and the result for them with a longer driver will be a far larger dispersion pattern and more off-center hits.

The term *face angle* is used to describe the positions of the clubface—square, closed, or open—when the club is seated naturally behind the ball, that is, with no manipulation by the hands of the golfer. Previously, 90 percent of all drivers were built with faces about two degrees open. Consequently, the average golfer couldn't quite figure out why he was hitting the ball to the right off the tee. A fully square face will appear a couple of degrees hooked or closed at address, which is what we are seeing more of these days in club making.

It is very important that you know what face angle you have on your driver. If you are a chronic slicer, you should consider using a driver with a slightly closed face. The player with the problem of hooking should consider a driver with a more open face. So, check the face angle of your driver this way. Let it lean against a wall and then stand about six feet away, directly opposite the toe of the club. If the toe appears to be laid back, you have an open clubface. If the heel area appears to be behind the toe, the face is closed. Remember, too, that if you are happy with the feel of your driver but believe your face angle is unsuitable for you, a good club maker can possibly alter the face angle. Sometimes that is a better solution to a driver problem than going to the expense of a new club. Also, there is something great about the feel of a familiar old driver that can never be replaced no matter how hard you try.

For years, men's conventional drivers had 11 degrees of loft, women's drivers 12 or 13 degrees of loft. While these lofts are still available, many drivers are built now with less than 11 degrees of loft. Sean Fister, National Long Driving champion for 1995, uses a driver with 3 degrees of loft! A loft angle of more than 11 degrees produces increased backspin, higher shots, less roll, and less distance.

We must be aware that the actual loft of a driver can be and is changed by the angle of attack on the golf ball. By playing the ball forward in the stance, the 11-degree driver could launch a ball at a 13- or 14-degree angle. By playing it back, an 11-degree driver may launch the ball at 9 degrees or less. So, if you are driving the ball too low, you might consider a driver with increased loft, say 12 or even 13 degrees. If you are hitting your drives too high and losing distance, you might want to change to a club with 9 or 10 or fewer degrees of loft. Short-hitting women need lofts greater than 12 degrees.

Lie angle refers to the angle the clubshaft makes when you are soling it naturally in preparation for your normal swing. When you *sole* your driver, it should rest on a spot one inch toward the heel of the club. A club that sits too far back on the heel will cause a pull to the left; one that, when soled, rests more toward the toe will cause a push to the right. Of course, the way you hold your hands on the club also has the final effect on lie angle. Hands held low tip the toe of the club up; hands held high bring the toe down. You must experiment to find the lie angle that suits your swing. Your professional can counsel you, and I recommend that you take his or her advice.

THE PROPER SWING WEIGHT FOR YOU

The term *swing weight* refers to the balance of the club in motion and defines the relationship between the shaft and the clubhead. It is measured on an arbitrary scale with band C being light, D heavier, and E the heaviest. The physical laws involved when you apply this to a club in motion are complicated. Suffice it to say that as a general rule a driver that is heavier in swing weight or total weight, or both, will tend to cause the golfer to lose clubhead speed and thus lose distance as well. Yet an unusually light driver can cause you to be too quick and can be hard to control. Lighter clubs may add distance to the shots of most golfers. But a few players actually get more distance with added head weight rather than reduced weight. Once again, it is one of those situations in which you must experiment for yourself to find the swing weight and overall weight that give you the best control and the best results.

Your club professional or any club repair shop can supply, at reasonable cost, strips of lead tape to determine whether you can handle a heavier, distance-producing swing weight in your driver. I recommend that you experiment with your driver clubhead in this way. Put a two-inch-long strip of the lead tape on the back of the club, above the sole plate, and center it directly behind the hitting area, spreading it from toe to heel. Hit about 10 drives to determine how the change in weight feels. Then add more lead strips, one at a time, and go through the same procedure. When you start hitting most of your drives to the right, you will have the signal that the swing weight has become too heavy for you to get the club through. Then, start removing the strips, again one at a time, until you find you can drive the ball with consistency. You'll have your answer in swing weight. Some players shift the weight toward the heel or toe of the clubhead to encourage a draw or fade. Additional weight on the back of the head toward the heel will encourage a slice; toward the toe, a hook.

Face depth refers to the distance between the sole and the top of the face of the driver. Standard face depth of most drivers today is one and five-eighths inches. There are many variations, of course: there are deeper faces and also shallow faces. The shallow-faced driver usually has a lower center of gravity and thus sends the ball at a higher angle. This is one of the features of the Tight Lie clubs by Adams Golf for fairway shots. As a general rule, the deeper the driver face, the longer the flight of the ball with the same loft angle. With the lighter materials for clubheads allowing for larger sizes, the opportunity for greater face depth is more prevalent. Many golfers choose the deeper-faced drivers because they like to see a lot of face and a lot of clubhead mass, which in their cases leads to a feeling of latent power. My suggestion again is that you try both kinds, deep-faced and shallow, and find the one that works best for you.

The *weighting of the clubhead* refers to the way weight is built into the head design or added to the clubhead. The club with weight at the back will produce a higher trajectory than the club with foreweighting. It is another one of those decisions you should make after experimenting.

Face progression refers to the distance your clubface protrudes in front of the center line of your driver. That line can also be behind the center line, in what is called an "offset" clubface. Basically, the more progression, or distance in front of the center line, the higher the launch angle will be. Offset drivers hit the ball lower.

The term *facing* refers to the radius on the club face from heel to toe. It helps the golfer to compensate for mishit shots. It causes the player's ball to start farther to the left on shots hit in the heel. The spin imparted to the ball then tends to bring the shot back to the fairway center. Ten inches is "standard radius" on a driver and has been the measurement observed by most manufacturers.

Taking all of these factors into account is a complicated matter but one that is solvable if given enough time and attention. We have to trust the manufacturers to produce the most efficient club designs, and generally they do. But you need to be aware of all the factors that influence your decision on the proper driver for you, that killer driver that carries your ball straight and far down the fairway. It may be a long search, but the result will be worth all the trouble.

SHAFT MATERIALS

In the early days golf shafts were made of hickory. Hickory was strong and flexible but was subject to torque, the force that causes the clubface to twist the shaft, particularly upon impact with the ball. Golfers in the days before steel shafts were truly magicians in the way they could maneuver the clubhead and the ball in spite of the torque in the shaft. This was particularly true since the amount of torque was not consistent from one shaft to the next. It was said that Tom Stewart, the old Scottish club maker, inspected several thousand different shafts before he chose a matched set of them for Robert T. Jones in the 1920s. Incidentally, that set is on display in

Far Hills, New Jersey, at the USGA headquarters and museum. Examples of very early wooden-shaft club making can also be seen at the World Golf Village in Florida. When the steel shaft came into general use in the late 1920s, the improvements in the problem of consistent response and reduction of torque outmoded the hickory shaft in a few short years.

Club makers continued to seek new materials for the clubshaft, looking for lighter weight with strength so that the weight removed from the shaft could be built into the clubhead. This would allow more power to be delivered to the ball.

Today, shafts of graphite are flooding the marketplace from a surprisingly large number of manufacturers. Graphite is lighter by several ounces than its standard counterpart in steel, although some superlightweight steel shafts are challenging that claim. Some players find that while they might hit with a graphite-shafted club a greater distance than they can with a steel shaft, the direction may be harder to control. This may be more true in the irons.

Perhaps there's a space age material down the road that weighs next to nothing, has no torque, has the proper flexibility, and will give us all 300-yard drives with little effort.

Titanium Clubheads

Titanium is a strong, low-density, highly corrosion-resistant, lustrous white metallic element used to alloy metals for lightweight strength and high temperature stability.

Developed for use in the aircraft industry, where light metal weight and strength are desirable, titanium came into the manufacture of golf clubs with a resounding "bang" when Callaway Golf introduced its new model driver "Big Bertha" in 1994.

Why titanium? Let's look at titanium's numbers: atomic weight 47.90, melting point 1,660 degrees Celsius, density 4.51 grams per cubic centimeter. Put simply, a clubhead made of titanium can be much larger than one made of steel (for example, Callaway's latest model driver measures 250 cubic centimeters, 25 percent larger than the steel model, yet it is 10 percent lighter).

The fact is that bigger golf clubs are more forgiving on off-center hits. Although a larger clubhead is subject to more aerody-

Lighter materials like titanium have made it possible
to increase the size of the
clubhead without adding
weight. This distributes
the weight over a greater
perimeter area, which
should contribute to
greater accuracy but not
necessarily to longer
distance.

The same holds true
for irons.

namic drag, the use of long, lightweight shafts (45 inches as
opposed to 43 $^1/_2$ inches), standard for most titanium drivers, produces higher speed at impact, and higher speed at impact means
greater distance. On the other hand, it is also true that the longer
the shaft, the harder it is for the golfer to hit the golf ball on the
"sweet spot" of the face. Perimeter weighting, that is, the building
of a clubhead with the weight around the outer edges of the face as
well as behind the center, reduces torque in off-center hits and
therefore produces less errant results with an off-center hit.

Presently, there are 38 different golf manufacturers producing
titanium drivers. The cost runs from as much as $1,400 for a
Japanese model to less than $250 for a small American company's
offering. Incidentally, if you think metal-headed drivers are of only

recent use, you should be aware that when Bob Hamilton defeated Byron Nelson in the 1944 PGA Championship at Manito Golf and Country Club in Spokane, Washington, he was using an aluminum-headed driver that had been manufactured for him by Reynolds Metals.

Before you buy a titanium driver, be sure to "road-test" a number of different clubs before you make your final decision. A test panel for *Golf* magazine recently found that there were many differences between the various clubs: the look of the head, the soundness of the hit (a few players complained of a "tinny" sound), the lie angle, the length of the shaft, the proper size grip for your hand, and, overall, your complete satisfaction with one of the most expensive toys of your golf career.

GOLF BALLS

All officially sanctioned golf balls must meet design and initial velocity specifications laid down and enforced by the United States Golf Association. There are variations in the construction, design, and compression of balls that will enable a golfer to pick up a few extra yards by using the ball that fits his swing.

Have you seen the ads on television or in magazines with fellows running around in white lab coats and holding clipboards while measuring golf shots on a lined field? Their company claims by official test to have the longest ball. But so do several other companies. How can that be true? Is someone lying? Not necessarily. It's just that they are giving you selected test results, the conditions under which their ball comes out the best. This is controlled either by trajectory, club selection, velocity chosen, or wind conditions. For example, one ball may go farther with a five-iron than another ball, but not as far under high-velocity driver conditions.

What about the ads for "super balls" from some firm you have never heard of at some post office box number? If such a ball were manufactured, it would be in violation of the rules. Your distance, like your score, should be honest.

Basically, there are four different methods of manufacture at this time. The first is the solid ball, made of a mixture of durable synthetic rubber materials. The ball won't cut, but because it is hard to put backspin on a solid ball it is more difficult to stop on approach shots to greens. The second type is the two-piece ball with a solid synthetic core covered with a synthetic cover. This is a big seller because of its toughness and the longer distance it gets with irons. The third type is the wound ball with a thin artificial balata cover or a cover of similar feel. In the center of the ball is a small ball filled with a dense liquid and wrapped with hundreds of yards of thin rubber bands wound tightly around that center. The three-piece ball feels softer than the solid ball and stays on the clubface longer, increasing the golfer's ability to spin the ball and thus control it better. Wound balls cut easily, so they are not favored by the higher-handicap player who mishits them too frequently. They are gradually being reduced in numbers sold and may disappear from use entirely in the near future.

The fourth type of ball is both multicovered and multicentered, a four-piece product. The result is a ball with more of the characteristics of a three-piece ball but with the cut-proof advantage of the two-piece.

The dimple pattern on the balls affects the way the ball is lifted in the air aerodynamically. Balls with large dimples will carry 10 percent farther when the wind is behind them because they will attain a higher trajectory. Balls with small, shallow dimples will stay lower, bore into the wind, and carry 10 percent farther when hit into the wind.

One of the most important discoveries about golf balls has been the fact that altering the depth, the size, and the number of dimples can change the flight characteristics considerably. In the early days dimpling was done almost at random, as the Scottish golf ball maker took a hand tool and struck the surface of the golf ball in order to roughen it. The earliest of golfers had found, probably by accident, that a golf ball that had been scratched by being hit into the brambles or marred by being struck badly a number of times actually went straighter than a smooth golf ball that had no surface blemishes.

Today, most balls come in compression ratings of 80, 90, and 100. There are some made with lower ratings for driving ranges. According to research data, all of these balls will go approximately the same distance but will simply feel harder or softer to the player. My experience is that a harder ball will go a bit farther for the big hitter, even though research doesn't bear that out.

The average golfer will get better feel from an 80 or 90 compression ball than he or she will get from a 100 compression ball. In cold weather it is often advisable to switch to a lower compression ball. Cold weather causes some loss of distance, but you will lose less distance with a lower compression ball, and it will feel better when hit. Just as you must find the driver that fits you, so too must you find the golf ball that works best for you.

TESTING BALLS AND CLUBS WITH THE MECHANICAL DRIVING MACHINE

A number of years ago the golf equipment manufacturers realized it was becoming increasingly important that they have uniform,

Balls come in different compression levels, such as 90 and 100. From a feel standpoint, this is a measure of hardness, with lower numbers being softer. The difference as far as distance is concerned is negligible.

extremely precise testing devices so they could study and compare the design, durability, initial velocity, and various other flight characteristics of golf balls as well as the performance of clubs. The results have been fruitful, to say the least. Many benefits have resulted from the testing that has been done on these driving machines.

The mechanical driving machine used by the USGA is called "Iron Byron" because the classic swing of Byron Nelson was photographed and used as the model by the design engineers. Incidentally, in the prime years of his game, Byron Nelson's backswing did not take the club to a position parallel with the ground, the 270-degree mark, but stopped at 265 degrees. So the machine's backswing stops at the 265-degree mark, which, by the way, is still about 20 degrees farther back than what the typical high-handicap player achieves. The machine works on a two-lever system similar to the motion of a human being. The clubhead is started at the top of the backswing from a fixed position at 5 degrees from parallel to the ground, and the "arm" mechanism is connected so as to provide a double-lever action that delivers a "delayed-release hit" as the clubhead reaches the ball.

The machine works by various electrical and pneumatic machinery that can be adjusted to a range of clubhead speeds and adapted to different lengths of golf clubs. When golf clubs are tested, the ball is hit in several different places on the clubface so one can tell the effectiveness of the design and where the sweet spot is.

Testing has uncovered many important facts about what happens when a golf clubhead strikes a golf ball at speeds of up to 170 miles an hour. With high-speed photography the ball can be seen flattening against the clubface and then springing back into shape and flying away at a tremendous initial velocity. By marking the ball with latitude and longitude lines, the spin rate of the ball can be determined with great accuracy from high-speed photography. The spin rate has a great deal to do with the golfer's ability to control the ball.

What advice can we give golfers in general about choosing a golf ball to fit their games? In our opinion, everyone should find the golf ball that suits his or her own "feel." While the top brands of balls perform reasonably close to one another on overall distance tests, there is a difference in flight characteristics. The results of tests on Iron Byron show a considerable difference between golf balls of different types and from manufacturer to manufacturer. Some golf balls are not constructed under as rigid manufacturing standards as others. That's why sometimes you'll find one golf ball that differs considerably from the others in that it has a much larger dispersion factor. If you had 10 successive identical drives with that brand of golf ball, you might find a 20-yard variation in those drives from side to side and from the shortest to the longest. But stiff competition has caused improvements.

There is no doubt that much of the low scoring of today can be attributed to improvements in the golf ball. There have also been significant advances in club design.

One of the important discoveries that was made is that the ideal launch angle for a drive is about nine degrees. It's been found that drives at that angle carry farther and roll farther than at any other lesser or greater angle. This means that the average golfer should adjust his or her swing and club loft so that the ball gets out on the nine-degree angle.

How does one measure his or her own launch angle? It's not too difficult, really. By using simple mathematics you can figure out that a ball launched at a nine-degree angle will reach a height of 3 feet at a distance of 20 feet, and a height of 6 feet at 40 feet. You can stick a couple of poles in the ground at 20 feet or 40 feet and stretch a piece of string between them, 3 feet or 6 feet above the ground. Then drive your golf ball between the poles and have a companion observe whether your drives are going over or under the string. You can tell very quickly what adjustment, if any, you need in your swing or the loft of your clubface.

Should the driver's face angle be nine degrees in order to put the ball out at a nine-degree angle? Oddly enough, no. This varies with the player's angle of approach to the ball and the flexibility of the shaft. The face loft could be greater than nine degrees, or less. Also, players with extremely high clubhead velocities may need less clubface loft since they produce more ball spin, which makes the ball climb to a higher apex in its trajectory.

Our advice to all golfers is to buy the best in up-to-date golf clubs. Be sure to get clubs that fit your swing, are the right length, and have the right lie, the right thickness of grip, the right overall weight, the right swing weight, and most important, the right shaft. Use a good golf ball with a feel you like. Hit the ball squarely on the face of the club (check that by using face decals). Then work on increasing clubhead speed by doing the exercises we recommend. There's no doubt that Iron Byron hits the ball much farther with his 120-mile-an-hour swing than he does with his 88-mile-an-hour swing!

> "You do have to have a lot of natural ability to hit the ball 275 yards. This is something that takes a certain combination of reflexes, strength, coordination, and above-average timing."
>
> ARNOLD PALMER

5
Driving for Distance

GREAT FEATS OF DISTANCE

Who do you think has the longest drive in the golf record books? Was it made by Jack Nicklaus, Sam Snead, Jimmy Thomson, George Bayer, John Daly, or Tiger Woods? No, it was made by Kyle Wheelas of Beaumont, Texas. He once drove a ball that landed in the open cockpit of an airplane heading for Houston. When that ball came down it had traveled 90 miles. No doubt that drive caused a great deal of talk at the 19th hole.

Distance is inevitably the main topic of conversation when golfers talk about their efforts on the links. Commemorative monuments have been erected on the spots where great drives came to rest. Golf ball manufacturers constantly aim their advertising campaigns to appeal to your distance ego. Millions of words have been written in books and magazines about driving length, and countless more have been spoken over postmatch refreshments concerning one of golf's most fascinating phenomena—distance.

Here are a few stories about length that may give you something to shoot for.

Discounting Wheelas's "trick shot," there have been many other driving feats that must be placed in the prodigious category. Consider Mr. T. A. V. Haydon, an Englishman, who in 1934, while playing at the East Devon Club, accomplished the following driving feats in one day: (1) drove to the edge of the 9th green, 465 yards downhill; (2) overdrove the 11th hole, a 358-yard uphill dogleg; and (3) drove just short of the 17th, 450 yards downhill. Not bad for a single day's outing. Or how about his fellow countryman, W. Smithson, the professional from Sitwell Park who one year later drove the 416-yard 2nd green from the championship tee? In comparison that may not seem so remarkable, except that he carried a dyke that crosses the fairway at 380 yards, from which the terrain of the hole runs steeply uphill to the green! (There was a following wind, but its velocity was not recorded.)

For these gargantuan drives, course and wind conditions have to be quite favorable. Most of the seemingly superhuman efforts had a bit of help from Mother Nature: dry, hard fairways, a favorable wind, and in the two cases just mentioned, the smaller British 1.62-inch ball used at that time, which traveled farther.

A phenomenal driving feat performed in this country with the larger American ball was Nebraskan Bob Mitera's record hole-in-one. At the Omaha Miracle Hills Golf Course (what an appropriate name!) he aced the 10th hole, 444 yards distant! He was aided, however, by an estimated 50 mph wind gust, an October fairway hardened by a dry summer, and a downhill slope 290 yards from the tee. Even so, this was still a major feat for a guy who stands only 5 feet 6 inches tall and weighs 165 pounds.

From reading this you may be thinking that you're not getting the distance from your driving that you should. But under normal conditions the records set in the past, even by Tour players, are within a normal human being's firepower. Statistics compiled at a U.S. Open Championship 15 years ago revealed that the average distance of the drives on the opening and closing holes for the greatest golfers in the world was 244.3 yards. This compared with an average of 253.4 yards in a regular PGA Tour event. Certainly, the course, its conditioning, and hazards play a definite part in those figures. But today's players, with better equipment and more vigorous physical training, are producing bigger numbers. At the 1997 U.S. Open, the average drive was 268.3 yards, and the leader, Tiger Woods, averaged 306! An interesting statistic from that same Open is that Jack Nicklaus, the former "big hitter" on Tour, ranked 67th out of 84 in the field with an average of 259.9 yards. An example of what age does to power.

Big drives that are made in the heat of competition seem more significant because of the circumstances. Here the name players begin to appear, the ones that you have heard and read about. George Bayer, for example, from a generation ago, had an actual measured drive of 420 yards in the Las Vegas Invitational in 1953. He had proof that it was that long because the ball struck a spectator and the distance was measured for use as future evidence in case of litigation.

But the men can't corner the market completely on driving records, for there have been a few women who also could sock the ball pretty well. The longest ace for women is a mind-boggling 393 yards made by Marie Robie of Woolaston, Massachusetts, at the Furnace Brook Golf Course in 1949. But for consistent distance, Mildred "Babe" Didrikson Zaharias took a back seat to few men and women in her era. Her length constantly amazed the golf spectators who were accustomed to seeing the ladylike pats of most women golfers. When Babe was asked how she could give the ball such a ride, she replied characteristically, "Why, kid, I just loosen my girdle and let her fly." Babe hit many a great tee shot in her career, but considering the circumstances, one of her more unbelievable performances happened before she had even entertained the notion of entering the golf world. On the day after the Olympic track and field meet in 1932, in which Babe had competed in three events, she accompanied some sportswriters to a local course for her very first round of golf. With borrowed clubs, she amazed her playing companions by reaching in two shots the apron of the 523-yard 17th hole against the wind!

When Babe left the golfing scene, having succumbed to cancer, the long-ball title was assumed without contention by lithe and strong Mickey Wright. Mickey once drove 10 yards past a 385-yard hole in Texas. Although she was aided by those two old helps—wind (40 mph) and that Texas hardpan—the performance still must rank as one of the all-time great feats for women. Today, it's Laura Davies from Great Britain who amazes the galleries. In a recent skins game she reached a 530-yard par-five with a drive and three-iron with no helping wind.

Many great hitters have written down their secrets on length, like Jimmy Thomson, the "King of Clout" in the 1930s, with his *Hit It a Mile* instruction book. In an official driving contest he averaged 324 yards for 10 shots. In the 1935 U.S. Open at treacherous Oakmont, Jimmy was home with a drive and a three-wood in two consecutive rounds on the 610-yard 12th hole.

But Thomson was always amazed that when he went on tours of the United States to demonstrate his driving prowess, in small towns from Keokuk, Iowa, to Butte, Montana, he would find unknown golfers, guys you never heard of, who could hit it farther than he could. No matter how long you are, there always seems to be somebody somewhere who can hit it a little farther. Even today's male leading long hitter, Tiger Woods, who reached the par-five 15th at Augusta twice with a nine-iron on his second shot in his victory year of 1997, says he knows other guys you never heard of who hit it right with him for distance.

One of the game's longest hitters of a few years back worked very hard to develop the strength in his left side until it was stronger than his right. His name was Clarence Gamber, a slugging sensation from Pontiac, Michigan. This 190-pound professional once entered a driving contest by walking to the tee in his sport coat and street shoes. He borrowed a driver from someone standing by, and after being told where the farthest shot had been hit, promptly took one swing and out-flew the previous best effort by 15 yards. He strode off saying, "Let them shoot at that for a while." Strength was also an important factor in the great driving ability of turn-of-the-century Englishman Ted Ray. Though his style was crude by modern terms, at a strong 220 pounds he could throw a great deal of force into his efforts. He ably demonstrated

How do you stack up with the long hitters? Clubhead speed is the factor that training for greater distance seeks to most directly affect. Here is a simple speed and distance measuring device, a Swing-o-Meter, which simply snaps onto your clubshaft.*

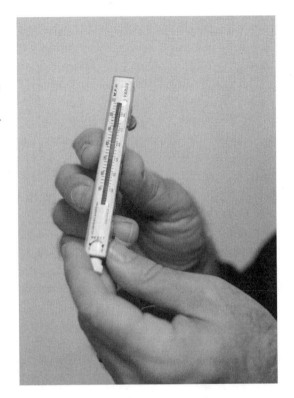

this on one occasion while playing with three other great champions, all pretty fair country hitters—Harry Vardon, Alec Smith, and Johnny McDermott. On a 268-yard hole with an elevated green, the other three players hit drives several yards short into the rain-soaked bank. Ray chose a cleek (the equivalent of our one-iron) and carried the green 10 feet from the flag!

But strength and size alone are not the only answers. The best example I know of is the case of a former Big Ten football player. At 6 feet 5 inches and 240 pounds you would think he could drive a golf ball across Lake Michigan, but he couldn't. In fact, he could hardly hit it the length of the club's swimming pool. Naturally, this was a constant source of irritation to the big fellow. You can just

*Available from Golf Around the World, The Learning Aids Company, (800) 824-4279

imagine how he felt whenever he went out to play with someone new and was told, "Gee, a guy as big as you should be able to hit that little ball out of sight," and, of course, he couldn't do it.

The crowning blow to Mr. Big Ten's ego came after a disappointing nine-hole round when he dragged himself to the practice tee to try again to cure the anemic condition of his driver. Try as he might, with every muscle quivering, he couldn't seriously threaten anything beyond the 200-yard marker. As he neared the bottom of his range bucket, he heard the solid crack of balls behind him and turned to see the district junior girls champ, all 115 pounds of her, flushing her drives out to a spot easily 10 yards beyond his best efforts. That did it! He stomped away from the clubhouse, his ego irreparably damaged. He gave up golf and now has become a good gin rummy player. But there are some other, wiser choices he could have made to still be happily playing golf. One of those would have been learning how to generate more clubhead speed. Flexibility is one of the answers.

While flexibility is the least discussed factor influencing distance, it obviously abounds in our younger golfers and is present as well in many of our longest-driving adult hitters. One physically unimpressive young collegian who could really bomb the ball was little known Henry Fogg of Fresno State College. This thin, slope-shouldered young man only a little over six feet tall would stand no chance of being picked from a crowd as one of golf's longest—but he was. Although not muscle-beach strong, he possessed specific strength to produce rotary speed, fantastic flexibility, and great timing. His superlate hit allowed him to accomplish feats regularly that few long hitters would even attempt. On the 11th hole at Pasatiempo in Santa Cruz, California, he regularly carried a barranca over 300 yards distant. In an NCAA meet in Eugene, Oregon, he topped his tee shot on the final hole, a 475-yard par-five, then flew a three-wood to the center of the green, a measured 315 yards. Henry Fogg demonstrated convincingly that size isn't the only answer to distance.

An interesting observation is that the golf swing and the baseball swing have many similarities. If a baseball player understands

the golf swing, it can help him with his batting. The late great
New York Yankee Mickey Mantle, a long-ball hitter in his own
game, once came into Kansas City in a bad slump. The first night
he went without a hit in three times at bat. That evening after the
game he went out to dinner and was talking about the golf swing
with a friend, who told him he needed to apply his golf fundamentals to his hitting. Specifically, he was told to stay back of the
ball or, as they say in baseball, not to stride too quickly into the
ball. Mick went out the next night and got three hits, and he went
on to win the Triple Crown of batting for the year. Mick later said
that the conversation about the golf swing was the turning point
in his season. By understanding the golf swing, he helped himself
in his hitting. If I am teaching a golfer who is tight, with an artifi-
cial-looking motion, I often suggest he simply make a horizontal
baseball swing and repeat the same swing with the body inclined
for a golf shot. They are similar.

I'd like to tell you about what I think was the most pressure-
filled long drive in the history of golf. Imagine if you were in a
long-driving contest and had to hit your drive 348 yards to win,
and furthermore, you had just *one* ball to do it?

That was the situation that confronted Evan "Big Cat"
Williams in one of the early long-driving contests held at Pebble
Beach. Evan was in his early 30s, slim, 6 feet 6 inches tall, and
weighing 205 pounds. He used a 44-inch, extra-stiff graphite-
shafted driver weighing $14^1/_2$ ounces, $1^1/_2$ ounces heavier than the
norm at that time. His driver had nine degrees of loft. The final
round for the 10,000-dollar prize was actually worth 100,000
dollars or more to Big Cat in driving exhibition money. One of
the earlier contestants, Cotton Dunn, had already driven the ball
$347^1/_2$ yards, and it appeared that he would be the winner, especially since Big Cat's first four drives were errant or short. He was
down to his last ball. One swing left—one that had to be perfect
under tremendous pressure.

Evan himself tells how he did it in his book, *You Can Hit the
Golf Ball Farther.* He says, "The preparation I had done for the
contest had given me the confidence I could produce the longest

drive so I didn't feel any pressure to do anything different. I had a technique I knew I could count on. I told myself to stay relaxed, take it back nice and slow, trust my swing. I took a few quick breaths. I find that taking a few short breaths sometimes is more relaxing than taking one deep breath. Anyway, it worked!" With Dunn's wife and daughter holding their hands over their eyes, Evan Williams hit his final shot 353 yards to become the national champion for the second straight year, thus securing his place in long-drive history.

HOW FAR DO THE PROFESSIONALS DRIVE THE BALL?

The PGA Tour keeps accurate statistics on many phases of the players' games. For the purposes of this book, the statistics on both length of drives and accuracy (driving the ball in the fairway) are most interesting. Four of the longest drivers on the PGA Tour as of this writing are in the top 20 money leaders: Tiger Woods at 294.1 yards is first in both money and driving, Scott McCarron is second in driving and 17th in money, Phil Mickelson is third and 19th, and Davis Love III is sixth in driving at 280.9 and 10th in money. Having the ability to hit long distances is an advantage! Possessing that extra power is a great advantage if it is used properly. For very long hitters there is the advantage of being able to gear back to use a driving iron or fairway wood, thus being more accurate. It also means being able to hit shorter irons to greens. Reaching greens in regulation is highly correlated to good scoring, and hitting greens with short irons after a long drive is a lot easier.

We should strive to hit our drives as far as we can but with enough control to place them in the fairway most of the time. When we start getting uncontrolled distance, it is time to throttle back at a moderate sacrifice of distance. But for most of you readers, throttling back is not the problem. We're more concerned about adding distance so that you can reach the green in regulation figures and putt for more birdies.

HOW TO PRACTICE DRIVING

I know you are serious about improving the length of your drive. I would like to suggest that you consider a regular routine of practice driving in order to permanently incorporate into your swing the fundamentals of practical, long, straight driving.

Of great importance are your tools. You have your favorite driver, we will assume, but you may have some other driver you wish to try. You need test balls as well. I recommend that you procure a dozen golf balls of the same make that you are accustomed to using. If you are comparing two drivers, go out on the course alone late in the evening and take driver A to hit the number ones and threes in your dozen and driver B to hit the twos and fours. Play two to three holes, hitting all dozen balls on each hole, and chart the dispersion and distance. You'll get a distinct feeling that either one is better than the other, or that they are pretty much interchangeable.

When you head for the practice tee the ideal situation is to be able to practice with as little distraction from other golfers as you can. Some people find that practice in the early morning is the most rewarding. The dew is sometimes a problem but the disadvantage of the wetness is offset by the advantages of being fresh physically and usually alone on the tee. Another good time is late in the evening. It will depend upon your work schedule. If you are a commuter in a major city, perhaps a lunchtime session at a range or an indoor facility is your only answer.

Always practice driving to a target. Visualize a fairway using the distance flags, markers, or trees on the range. Go through your routine and see if you can put 14 out of 18 drives into the fairway. Mix in some shots, simulating dogleg holes or out-of-bounds as might happen on the course. The closer you can make your practice resemble the actual game, the more effective it will be.

Before you start your driving practice, remember to go through the warm-up exercises shown here. I call them the "no ball" warm-up. I recommend them highly when you have arrived at the first tee without hitting practice balls. In fact, anytime you intend to make a full swing at a golf ball, you should warm up first. If you do not, you may incur serious muscle strain. Whenever you add speed to a physical task like lifting, throwing, or swinging, the risk of injury seriously increases if you don't warm up.

When you are warmed up satisfactorily, and not before, you may begin your driving practice. Spill your golf balls about 15 feet behind the area from which you will be driving. The idea behind this is that you will be forced to take your time between shots by walking back to the pile and getting your next ball.

Sometimes there is no opportunity to hit balls to warm up before you tee off. The following series is a "no-ball warm-up" to get the body ready for a full swing. Start with two wedges, short swings building to longer ones.

Next, stretch the back muscles with the club hooked
in your elbows.

Use your full body rotation.

Then place the club across your upper back and wind over the right leg.

Finish all the way over the left leg.

Hook your thumbs over the shaft, raise your arms behind you, and turn again, back . . .

. . . then through, using your full turn.

Here's a demonstration of
shoulder flexibility at age
62 (pulling the club all the
way over my head and
down the back with the
arms straight).

If you are working primarily on driving with control, put two clubs on the ground to represent a path to your target. Also place one club parallel to your feet. But do not, and I cannot emphasize this point too strongly, do *not* make a swing without consciously aiming at a target or landing area. Golf is a target game. You should always be aiming at that flag, trying to hole out the shot, or at some area to put the ball into a favorable position.

Now, proceed to drive your golf balls one after the other, all at the target. Take your time between shots. Stand behind the ball before each shot and visualize your line to the target. Then work on your body and clubface alignment by referring to the parallel clubs on the ground. This is critical, since long drives with a good swing that go in the wrong direction due to misalignment will eventually require you to alter your swing and become less effective.

I happened to watch Jack Nicklaus practice his driving when he was playing at his best. Jack was working on his setup. On one

The "power path" has the clubhead approaching the ball slightly from the inside. Note that the intended flight line and foot line are parallel.

occasion he stepped away from his ball three times to check his body alignment. Then he took a club and put it across his chest in line with his target to make certain his alignment was correct. If Jack can do this and feels he must do this, so can you.

As you practice, try to work on one segment of the swing at a time. Let's say you are trying to slow down your swing. You have been swinging too fast and losing control at the top of your swing. Work on this thought as you make your swings. Say to yourself, "slow back," even to the point of pronouncing "slooooooooow back" while you are in the act of taking the club away. One PGA professional uses the words *golf swing* to improve tempo. But he notes that in his mind the word *golf* is in capital letters and spaced G-O-L-F to slow the backswing and the word *swing* is in small letters and closer together to get speed in the forward motion.

Note how things went during the practice session. Write down what is working. I believe in keeping track of my practice sessions on the different aspects of the game. Many serious golfers keep diaries. I recommend that you keep one. You will be better able to see progress in achieving longer distance on your drives. It will give you a great deal of satisfaction to enter into your diary that today you were driving 10 yards farther than you were when you first began your practice program.

WHY YOU MUST LEARN TO DRAW THE BALL FOR MORE DISTANCE

The United States Golf Association conducted many interesting experiments with their mechanical driving machine. One such experiment attempted to determine whether there was any substantial difference in the results of a golf swing that caused a *fade*, or left-to-right action on the ball, in contrast to a swing that caused a *draw*, or right-to-left action. The tests proved that there are appreciable distance benefits drawing the ball and serious detriments in fading it. A controlled draw with a driver travels farther than a fade.

The driving machine was set to produce a clubhead speed of 90 miles an hour, which is the speed of an average 5- to 10-handicap player. The clubface of the driver was adjusted one and one-half degrees open for the fade, one and one-half degrees closed for the draw. The two swings were identical in regard to attack angle and swing path.

The opening and closing of the clubface produced shots that traveled an average of 18 yards to the right or left of the center of the fairway. But the startling fact that emerged from these tests was that the draws rolled 16 to 17 yards farther after landing, while the fades rolled less than 9 yards. The explanation for these results is that the faded shot is launched at a higher angle than the drawn shot. It has more backspin applied to it. There are also aerodynamic effects of "lift" and "drag," both of which are increased. The faded ball sails higher and curves to the right

Here's a visual explanation (a Shot-Maker) for a draw or hooking-type shot that has less backspin than a fade or slice and more distance. The face is closed relative to the path. Make the path come from the inside to slightly outside your aim line with the face square and you'll have this preferred shape.

because of the initial clockwise spin imparted by the open clubface, but it does not travel as far. When the clubface is closed at
impact, the opposite happens. The loft of the club is decreased, the
launch angle is lower, less backspin is created, and the forward
speed is increased. While backspin is necessary to keep the ball in
the air, apparently the effect of less backspin is more than offset
by the increase in forward speed, so the drawn ball carries farther.

Frank Thomas, USGA's technical director, explains that "the
swing that produces a draw is more powerful than the swing that
produces a slice." The draw swing approaches the ball from inside
the target line on a more shallow and better angle.

The draw launches the ball with more forward speed and also
promotes greater accuracy and more consistency. When the amateur golfer makes a slice swing, he or she usually does it by coming at the ball from outside the target line and at a steeper angle.
The result is that the slicing action is increased, the loft and spin
on the ball are increased, and the ball flies higher, shorter, and
more to the right.

Gary shows John that when the left arm separates too far from the body it blocks
the return of the face to square and causes a distance-robbing slice.

The tests showed that the faded ball averaged 207 yards in carry, ballooning up due to greater backspin, and ran 9 yards for a total of 216 yards. The drawn drives carried 217 yards and ran 16 more yards for a total of 233 yards. So the obvious conclusion is that with a choice of drawing or fading the ball, the ordinary golfer seeking increased distance should work to develop a controlled draw.

Incidentally, the test showed that the straight shot travels as far as the draw or even slightly farther due to its staying in the air longer than the draw. Although we will work to hit every drive perfectly straight, we should realize that if we don't hit it straight, we should favor the draw.

THE EFFECT OF COURSE CONDITIONS AND THE ELEMENTS

Bad-weather golf can be described as play in any weather that is abnormal. It might be golf in unusually cold temperatures, golf in strong winds, golf in the rain, or golf in terrible heat. Whatever bad conditions you may encounter, you must be prepared to deal with them sensibly and, if it is at all possible, overcome whatever obstacle is placed in your path. You may be required to play under unpleasant conditions, but you must always remember that your competitors must play under them too. If you are better prepared than they, you will have an advantage over them, you will play in a more relaxed fashion, and you will probably win more often than you lose. But keep in mind, unusual conditions can drastically alter your normal distance.

Let's examine a few of the circumstances that can be considered conditions of bad-weather golf and decide what preparations you should make in advance to deal with them.

Rain

At some time in your life, possibly many times depending upon the climate in your locality, you will be caught in a sudden rainstorm. You must always be prepared not only for rain but also for the sudden drop in temperature that often follows a storm. So be sure you have a big golf umbrella with you at all times. A big one will give you the greatest protection from the elements. It should have a wooden or plastic handle to lessen the possibility of your becoming the target of a bolt of lightning.

You should also consider carrying one of those lightweight waterproof pullovers. If you play in club competitions where it is often necessary to continue to play in the rain, you certainly should have a complete rain suit. If you do buy a rain suit, it is wise to spend a few extra dollars and get a good one. The cheaper suits may bind your swing or not "breathe," making you perspire. And of first order, make sure that it truly will keep you dry.

The problem of playing in the rain and of playing in bad-weather gear is that the added clothing may hamper your swing, and your clubhead speed could be lessened. You will have to experiment and determine for yourself how much this will affect you. Let's say that you normally hit a five-iron 150 yards under dry, ideal conditions. Try some practice in the rain when you get your new rain suit. It is likely that the same five-iron swing in the rain will travel only 140 yards. So, you have to build into your swing a 6 to 7 percent loss-of-distance factor. But, knowing that you will customarily lose that much distance will help you choose the right club in the rain. You might decide that in general you need one club stronger than usual, so your thinking process might be "five-iron minus one club equals four-iron." A very important point about taking a stronger club than usual is that you do not, you *must* not, ease up on the shot. Sometimes knowing that you have a stronger club causes you to hit it a little easier than normal. My advice is that you use a mental trick and pretend you have your normal five-iron. Just hit the four-iron as if it is a five-iron, and you'll be most surprised at your success.

When you play in the rain, it is generally true that your best success lies in taking a stronger club than usual. This statement is not true, though, when you are coming out of heavy, wet rough. There you need to get the ball up quickly, even at the sacrifice of distance, so take a more lofted club than usual. Also, tee your ball a little higher for extra carry on the drive. When you are playing in the rain, the water gets between your clubface and the ball. You do not get the usual spin of the ball off the blade. So you must allow for loss of spin in your judgment of distance. From good lies or very light rough, the ball will fly farther—that, of course, is the shot known as a *flier*. From heavy rough it flies shorter.

It is useful to have waterproof shoes for your occasional bouts with rain or wet course conditions. Some of the golf shoes designed for wet weather can be uncomfortably hot on your feet. You may be faced with the dilemma of either having wet feet from water getting into regular shoes or hot feet from watertight shoes. Here, too, is another good reason for buying good golf equipment from the start. Cheap shoes are uncomfortable and are the first to leak.

One of the most important bits of advice is: keep your grips dry; if you can't hang onto the club, you can't take a good swing at the ball. Carry a dry towel draped on your umbrella struts for that purpose. Also carry extra gloves, so that you can switch from a wet glove to a dry one if you are forced to do so. There are some wet-weather gloves on the market that actually grip better when they are wet rather than dry. I always carry one for extreme conditions. There are also certain brands of grips that are very slippery when wet and others that are hardly affected.

The best advice I can give you about playing in the rain is to take it easy. Try to swing with as perfect a rhythm as you can. It is very important that you hit the ball purely in the rain. So, if necessary, shorten your backswing and be sure to swing within yourself, which means don't overswing and don't try to overpower the shot or try to hit it harder just because you are losing distance on your shots. Let the additional distance come from using a stronger club rather than a stronger swing.

Try to swing with rhythm in the rain. You will be surprised at your success. It is especially satisfying to beat the elements. You can do it if you approach the problem and work with the rain rather than allow it to beat you.

Wind

Playing in wind poses different problems. In driving against the wind the ball should be kept as low as possible, where it will be less exposed to the effect of the wind. When the wind is from behind, try to get the ball up higher than usual so the wind can exert a greater and longer effect on its flight.

One way to drive the ball in a lower trajectory is to widen your foot position and play the ball back farther in the stance than normal, toward the centerline between the feet. Try to have your hands ahead of the ball at impact. The backward placement of the ball and the forward movement of the hands may cause an open face at impact, so it is most important that the clubface be turned slightly counterclockwise, so it will appear to be "closed," to counteract these tendencies. How much correction you will need, you alone can tell by experimentation. Making your swing more level with the ball teed high or low will also lower your shot's trajectory. You can practice this low-driving maneuver on a windless day on the practice tee. I recommend that you do so. The ability to hit a low drive is a wonderful addition to your game. It will save many strokes.

With the wind behind you, the suggested corrections should be reversed; that is, the ball should be teed higher, a little farther to the left than normal, and the hands should be allowed to be behind the ball at impact in order to produce a higher launch angle with more loft and, therefore, more carry. Stand tall, go to the end of the grip, and make a full swing, but not one with any more effort than normal. With the ball forward be sure to transfer your weight strongly to the left or you will pull across your intended swing path.

CONSULT A PROFESSIONAL TEACHER

Since the early days with my first professional instructor, I have been an avid student of the game of golf. Many times when I have encountered minor problems with my golf swing I have consulted professional teachers, who were usually able to spot my error and correct it. If you have not been taught by a professional teacher of golf thus far in your career, I suggest that you seriously consider doing so. Furthermore, I have some advice on the kind of teacher you should select.

You will find, as I did, that no two golf teachers are alike. There are *talkers*, who will talk the theory of golf to you, and there are *doers*, professionals who will watch you hit a few balls and then suggest a minor change in your swing that may work miracles for you. Or you may experience a "builder" teacher who wants to make your swing over completely. Any of these could be useful. You need to find a golf teacher who understands you, your personality, your character, your attitude, and your goals related to the game of golf.

Many teachers are accused of making so many changes in a pupil's swing that the pupil becomes hopelessly confused and "can't hit a thing." This may happen, especially if there are many faults to be corrected. All I can do is suggest that you be patient with your teacher and practice diligently the changes he or she suggests. Usually, the results are good, and if they are not the answer is, obviously, to seek out another teacher.

Once you have found a sympathetic and knowledgeable teacher, a person you like, go ahead and confide in him or her. Describe your tendencies, what you are trying to do, the thoughts that go through your mind when you prepare to hit a shot, and any physical problems. Don't be impatient and demand instant results. Most of us have muscles that have moved in the same way all our lives. Suddenly we are told by the golf teacher that we must move a little differently. It will take time, maybe months, to change the habits of a lifetime.

Here's another tip about choosing your golf teacher. Do not be surprised if it takes more than one instructor to find the right one. Your first instructor may prove to be ideal for you and you would never think of changing. That is great! On the other hand, you may find that at some time in your learning, you need another teacher who gives a different slant or approach to the game, one that solves some golf problems that weren't getting fixed. While you shouldn't be afraid to change teachers during your golf career, once you find the right one, make a commitment and stay put.

FINDING A GRIP

A good word of advice from someone who has experimented for years to find the best grip: don't fall in love with your grip if it is faulty. For some strange reason all of us seem to think that the way we learned to grip the golf club is *the way* and the only way to do it. The slightest suggestion of a change of the thumb position or rotation of either hand finds us fighting the change and perversely sneaking back to our first grip. Grip is a serious matter, in my opinion, and one that should be clearly understood if you wish to become the long driver this book intends you to be. I have suggested many exercises for your entire body. I have especially emphasized the building of strength in your left hand, left arm, and the left side. These limbs will inevitably become stronger day by day. Therefore, you will find that it will take more and more power in your right hand to take over and pass your left hand as you swing through the ball. Now, doesn't it make sense that if you are constantly gaining more strength in your left hand, the right hand should be able to apply more and more power at impact without breaking down the left? This is true, and the conclusion is that as you gain strength, you must be prepared to alter your grip to accommodate the change in your strength and flexibility. It may need to change again when your body changes, but if it does, change as few times as possible. Grip changes, while possibly being necessary, are not comfortable at first and take time to become so.

I recommend the practice of observing the great professional golfers in action. Nearly every section of the country is visited regularly these days by the PGA or Nike Tours. When there is an announcement of a coming Tour event near you, make every possible effort to attend. Be sure to go early enough to be able to watch the players warming up on the practice tee. When you go to a Tour event, go as a student with the intention of getting your money's worth in instruction from these great players. Many of the instructional ideas I have put into this book have come as a result of my observing some great players and adopting positive aspects of their techniques.

"Strength is a factor in golf. You're building and then applying leverage

with that club, and it comes from muscle power."

SAM SNEAD

6
The World's Longest Hitters

In the early days on the PGA Tour, driving contests were part of the weekly traveling show. They were all part of the hype for the coming event in those days before the advent of television, corporate sponsors, and tournament volunteer groups the size of Caesar's legions. For a first prize of only 50 to 100 dollars, the players would take three shots, trying to keep at least one in play and hoping that they didn't ruin their timing for the rest of the tournament. The longest hitters sorted themselves out pretty soon, so that you usually knew that one of about three or four individuals would win. Over four decades the long-driving favorites were Jimmy Thomson, Chick Harbert, Mike Souchak, and George Bayer.

What the public didn't always see were the locals—the exballplayer from the next county who could really move it, the college kid who grew up in town as a junior golfer and now had a reputation for being amazingly long, or the huge local police officer who had a 16 handicap but when he got hold of a drive it was gone, out of the county. That has changed today because the public is getting to see these people. The National Long Drive Competition has demonstrated that the longest hitters in the world aren't necessarily on the PGA Tour. In fact, most of them are not touring professionals. Of the winners over the past 23 years, only three were on the Tour. Many contestants were amateurs and others were nontouring golf professionals. From this event there has come more interest in long-hitting competitions and several years back the formation of "The 350 Club," comprising competitors who had hit the ball over 350 yards in an official driving event. The 350 Club has been a collection of some of the world's longest hitters, and was the marketing brainchild of golf professional and performer Mike Dunaway.

The Club's first event was the Slam-Am Pro-Am some years back at the Sands Hotel in Las Vegas. Amateurs played with the long hitters in a scramble event. First, a long-drive contest was held, and then a trick-shot show and exhibition. Dunaway booked the group in Puerto Rico, Atlantic City, and Japan—and they were on their way. It was in Japan that Dunaway observed the hardest-hit golf ball he'd ever seen. The contest was proceeding under less than ideal conditions with a light rain falling. Dunaway led the competition by almost 30 yards with a smash of 358 yards when Tom Winrow stepped up for a final turn and launched one 387 yards. The announcer was speechless for almost two minutes. Another interesting story of a similarly built competitor to Mike Dunaway is that of two-time National Long Drive champion Andy Franks.

ANDY "BALL PARK" FRANKS

Andy Frank's story is an amazing example of dedication and work. A two-time champion at 24 years of age, he had already defied the odds by having previously played golf for only four and one-half years. A 5-foot 11-inch, 210-pound bundle of muscle, Andy Franks did not just work on long-ball hitting but also on playing the game. Andy was a three-sport high school star in Florida but injured himself in his senior year in football. That turned him to golf. His longest official poke, besides the two in the national finals, was a 373-yard win in the Caribbean. He has driven several holes over 400 yards in length. Although he inherited a powerful body, he developed most of his strength while working the weights when training for football. His emphasis has been on losing some bulk across his chest and upper arms and working more on stretching, plus running and bicycling for cardiovascular fitness. Andy Franks has a straightforward approach to handling the pressures of long driving. "When you are the champ you are expected to do well. Everybody's shooting to knock you off. In that situation I do two things. One, I say, 'I know I can do it'; and two, I focus on good technique, the kind you'd use for hitting any good golf shots. I try to erase those other possible mental considerations—the crowd, the competition—from my mind."

His recommendation is to work on developing better technique. "I go to my professional, David Leadbetter, for lessons twice a week. I don't try to hit it long there. But as my swing gets better, the ball goes farther." He adds, "I see too many fat, out-of-shape golfers who are being handicapped in distance and the whole game by their poor conditioning."

JOHN McCOMISH

Another 350-yard performer and one of the better players to win the National Long Drive title was John McComish. A former Tour player (two other National Long Drive champions played the PGA Tour—Lon Hinkle in 1981 and Dennis Paulson in 1985), John was the PGA Tour's statistical leader in long driving one year with an average of 277.4 yards. But that feat pales in comparison to some of his other long-drive accomplishments. This 6-foot 6-inch, 240-pound mountain of a man with a plus-two handicap won the Long Drive Championship in 1978 and finished second in 1979 and fourth in 1980 and 1982. His longest poke in competition is 382 yards. One time on a 560-yard par-five, his drive stopped 30 yards short of the putting surface. He was a high school basketball athlete and college all-American golfer at Cal State

Northridge. In preparing for long-drive competition, John worked to increase his shoulder turn for more power. After a long-drive competition, John worked to return to his shorter playing swing. In addition to the bigger shoulder turn, he spread his feet farther apart in the long drive, taking the club back a little more slowly. The reason he spread his feet was to allow a wide enough base for an intentional extra body sway. He felt it was helpful in allowing him to create a wider arc, but it's not something he did when playing competitively.

John used the same driver for play and long driving: 44-inch length, eight-degree loft, dynamic X shaft, and a bulge of eight degrees. The fact that John competed with a regular-length club makes his feats even more impressive.

More recently has come the formation of the LDA (Long Drivers of America, Inc.), founded by long driver Randy Souza, who joined with former National Long Drive champion Art Sellinger in 1994 to conduct the U.S. Open Long Drive Championships.* Listed below are the winners of the national title since its inception in 1975 through 1997.

WINNERS OF THE NATIONAL LONG DRIVE COMPETITION

Year	Winner	Distance	Site
1975	Geoff Long	321 yards	Butler National Golf Club
1976	Evan Williams	301 yards	Congressional Country Club
1977	Evan Williams	353 yards	Pebble Beach Golf Club
1978	John McComish	330 yards	Oakmont Country Club
1979	Andy Franks	314 yards	Oakland Hills Country Club
1980	Scott DeCandia	295 yards	Oak Hill Country Club
1981	Lon Hinkle	338 yards	Atlanta Athletic Club
1982	Andy Franks	346 yards	Southern Hills Country Club
1983	Terry Forcum	307 yards	Riviera Golf Club
1984	Wedgy Winchester	319 yards	Shoal Creek Country Club

*Long Drivers of America, (888) 233-4654

1985	Dennis Paulson	323 yards	Firestone Country Club
1986	Art Sellinger	311 yards	Perdido Bay Country Club
1987	Mike Gorton	318 yards	Perdido Bay Country Club
1988	Jim Maynard	334 yards	Grand Bahama Princess Resort
1989	Scott DeCandia	327 yards	Grand Bahama Princess Resort
1990	Frank Miller	328 yards	Boca Raton Resort & Club
1991	Art Sellinger	326 yards	Boca Raton Resort & Club
1992	Monte Scheinblum	329 yards	Boca Raton Resort & Club
1993	Brian Pavlet	336 yards	Boca Raton Resort & Club
1994	Darryl Anderson	345 yards	Las Vegas Hilton
1995	Sean Fister	362 yards	Las Vegas Hilton
1996	Jason Zuback	351 yards	Las Vegas Hilton
1997	Jason Zuback	412 yards	Casa Blanca Golf Club

This group of athletes has some characteristics that seem specific to their success in long driving:

- Some are of average height (5 feet 10 inches to 6 feet) but are powerfully built, weighing over (sometimes well over) 200 pounds.
- Some are taller than normal (6 feet 2 inches to 6 feet 6 inches) and, although not necessarily powerful looking, have long body levers.
- Some are both tall and powerfully built (6 feet 5 inches, 265 pounds, as an example).

The age span for national champions ranges from Andy Franks, who won in 1979 at age 22, to Terry Forcum, who was a 41-year-old champ in 1983, but most are in their 20s and 30s. The current champions are using mostly various forms of graphite-shafted drivers that were in recent years around 46 to 48 inches long, but today are in many cases longer. Most of those who have become champions train regularly by using weights and stretching exercises plus individual specialized exercise routines.

SEAN "THE BEAST" FISTER

Typical of today's competitors is Sean "The Beast" Fister. One of the current long-drive specialists with some interesting stats, he is the 1995 North American Long Drive champion and was the North American record holder at 362 yards, 12 inches until the 1997 competition. He has unofficially driven the ball 441 yards, in competition 411 yards; he has hit it an amazing 348 yards from his knees, 341 yards left-handed, 223 yards with an eight-iron, and 287 yards with a putter. His clubhead speed has been measured at 162 miles an hour.

In the 1995 championship round Sean used a 48-inch Harrison shaft with 2.5 torque, a high kick point at 90 grams, and a Taylor Made tour burner head at three degrees loft. Currently, he is using the same head and shaft, with a Dargie Golf titanium head at three degrees loft.

Fister, like most of the competitors, trains rigorously. His program includes weight lifting designed specifically to strengthen the upper back, shoulders, triceps, forearms, wrists, and hands, as well as basic leg exercises to strengthen the legs. He does range-of-motion flexibility exercises with a weighted club of three to five pounds, and uses a cable pulley system that he designed specifically for developing explosive power.

JASON ZUBACK

Literally coming out of the woods from Drayton Valley, Alberta, Canada, in 1996 was Jason Zuback. The 28-year-old pharmacist is a former power lifter who could pass the 300-yard mark by age 16 but had never been seen before at the national finals. It didn't take long for Zuback to be noticed as he won in 1996 with a blast of 351 yards and in 1997 with a record launch of 412 yards, 3 feet, $3^{1}/_{2}$ inches! Zuback tours now throughout Canada and the United States exhibiting his talents and promoting long driving. His longest drive ever was a downwind noncompetitive rocket measured at 511 yards, and his longest measured carry is 430 yards, 10 inches!

Zuback works on strength, flexibility, and cardiovascular endurance. A typical in-season workout would be a stationary bike for 20 minutes, followed by 20 minutes of stretching and two to two and one-half hours of hitting balls. During the off-season (seven months in Canada) he focuses on weight training with the emphasis on muscles of the trunk region. Jason believes that visualization and relaxation, particularly in the hands and arms, are crucial to his good performance.

Two other current competitors deserving of special attention are Bobby Wilson and Brian Pavlet. Wilson, while never winning the national title, has been in the finals for 16 consecutive years and has never finished out of the top 10. That is some record! Pavlet won in 1993, and in 1997 he hit a drive of 435 yards at the championship but not in the final round. He is always a threat.

The President of Long Drivers of America,* Mr. Art Sellinger, was the 1986 national champion, has hit the ball 384 yards in competition, and averaged a phenomenal 325 yards in the national finals. PGA Tour star Lanny Wadkins says, "Art Sellinger is the longest driver of a golf ball day in and day out that I've ever seen."

Equipment changes seem frequent as technology keeps adding to the mix of design and materials. For example, Darryl Anderson, the 1994 National Long Drive champion at 345 yards, has used the following equipment over the past several years:

> 1990–1992: 44-inch metal-head Callaway eight-degree
> driver, R.C.H. 90 Callaway graphite shaft.
> 1993–1994: 7-degree Yonex Super A.D.X. 300 cc head,
> 48-inch Yonex stiff graphite shaft.
> 1995: 8.5-degree Crunch Golf Titanium Head, 48-inch
> Quadrax Thermo Composite 60-gram shaft.

The trend is definitely toward longer and lighter. Forty-seven-year-old Michael Hooper, the Senior Long Drive champion in 1996 at 334 yards and 1997 at 371 yards, makes for others and

---

*Long Drivers of America, (888) 233-4654

uses himself a 54-inch driver. And believe it or not, one 1997 contestant had a 63-inch driver, surpassing the 60-inch length of the one used by 1984 champ "Wedgy" Winchester.

Today's National Long Drive competition has become huge compared to its beginning in 1975. The RE/MAX corporation now sponsors the event, which in 1996 and 1997 was shown on ESPN on Christmas Day and was the highest-rated made-for-TV golf show telecast for each year. With RE/MAX's support, 5,100 individuals (including those in the senior division) have teed it up to blast away in over 200 local qualifying events, which lead to the districts and the 150,000-dollar finals.

So long driving not only pays on the course, as it has for John Daly and Tiger Woods, but is also gaining enough in popularity to pay in exhibitions and contests. One thing is for certain—the public has always been fascinated by the superlong hitter.

OBSERVATIONS FROM LONG DRIVERS

Here are some observations that champion drivers have made on why people are or are not long hitters:

- The reason average players lose distance is that they start with a bad grip and poor alignment and then end up at the top of their swings with too much weight on the left side (a reverse weight shift), giving them little punch to return to the ball.
- Most golfers simply need to develop better bodies if they want to hit the ball farther.
- Short hitters are too tense and too quick, particularly in their arms and hands. They should loosen up a little more and take a relaxed pace to the proper position at the top of their backswings to find their best distance.
- The average player is trying to think of the 25 details that he or she read in the latest golf magazine. Getting confused means getting tense and tied up. Be more natural and you'll be more relaxed.

The greatest speed will come from a rotational "slinging" sensation with a lack of tension in the arms and hands. This feeling is captured here by a training aid called Swing-Eez,* a soft ball attached to a handle and rubber tube.

*Available from Golf Around the World, The Learning Aids Company, (800) 824-4279

This product also teaches swing plane by touching the left shoulder and then the right as it's swung.

- Picking the club up on the backswing rather than sweeping it away encourages a downward glancing blow and less distance.

- Work on your back muscles to create a wide arc and a good arm swing. You need a good back to do that.
- Almost every player I have ever met has another 10 yards in that tee shot if he or she would just improve on technique. Swing improvements should come a little at a time, but as the swing improves, so will the distance.

Having the back to the target and the shoulders turned 90 degrees help create power.

- A lot of players don't set up correctly to hit the ball far. They have bad grips, poor aim, and a faulty stance and try to hit the ball hard on the backswing.

A good setup is a large part of a successful shot.

- Work on the sequence of motion in the swing. Get your links firing in the right order. Too many men overuse their upper body and get out of synch. It's a continuous flow, starting from below the waist.

Getting the proper sequence of motion is essential for the long drive.

- Hitting a golf ball long distances is an athletic feat. You must have strength, flexibility, and technique.
- The draw, or hooking ball, is preferred for greater distance.
- Equipment is a matter of choice. The same clubs don't work for everybody, but players with a great deal of power need extra-stiff shafts for better control, particularly with extra-long shafts.
- Thinking positively will help promote the desired feeling of "freewheeling."
- Strength and fitness training for golf will help you to hit the ball not only longer but better as well.
- Although exceptional long hitting is a gift, everyone can learn to hit longer.

And that's the bottom line. EVERYONE CAN LEARN TO HIT LONGER.

7
Random Insights and Selected Observations

Maybe a better title for this concluding section would be, WHAT ARE YOU WILLING TO DO? Life is full of sermonizers who love to tell you what you should do. I'm interested in motivating, not preaching. I'd simply like you to realize that you can be better and I'd like to help you create the spark to do it. So decide how important to you greater distance would be in playing better golf. If better golf is really very important to you, then allocate the time to get it done.

How far can you progress? Honestly, I don't know. No one, not even you, can predict that. But here are some clues. Remember, heredity is a factor. Your acquired nervous system, body proportion, innate strength, and flexibility all will place the eventual limitation on performance. Some people are naturally strong, flexible, or quick; others are not. However, we all can be stronger, more flexible, and quicker than we are at this moment. The answer for you may be primarily in swing technique. That's where a player can sometimes get the fastest results. The right drill, suggestion, or analogy from your professional instructor might add 15 to 20 yards instantly. If it's a technique change that you are contemplating or working on, give yourself time to allow it to become a habit and not just an idea. For example, developing additional wrist set on the downswing to create a more delayed hit in your link system (as opposed to casting your power away) is not instinctive. It takes time to feel it and a lot of successful shots to trust it.

Finally, recognize that long driving is an advantage only when it's effectively used. Golf is a game of numbers. A five with a slice will always beat a six by Tiger Woods. There are odds to deal with and circumstances to consider when you are allowing yourself freewheeling reign. A player like Nicklaus, who was certainly one of the longest in his early Tour days, was smart enough to recognize that a fairway wood or iron from the tee of a par-four or five was sometimes the better shot when you are considering the odds and playing for a living.

As we conclude this exploration of long driving, there are a few loose ends to tie up, things that don't belong anywhere else but that I wouldn't want you to miss.

HOW ABOUT SIZE?

It's not difficult to see how members of The 350 Club can hit it a long way. They, for the most part, are very large or powerfully built people. What about the smaller players? What do they have going for them? Early in his career (before his auto accident) the late Ben Hogan drove very long for a 5-foot 7-inch, 145-pound player. But as a contemporary observed, "He had bigger hands and arms than I did being 40 pounds heavier." The physical attributes that offset his limitations in stature were accompanied by a technique that employed one of the longest delayed-hit positions in history and an extremely wide extension at contact into the through swing.

Juan "Chi Chi" Rodriguez is but 5 feet 5 inches and 138 pounds; however, only a handful of big hitters on the Tour could stay up with him at his prime. He did not have big arms or hands, so how does one explain his distance? Again—a late release, more than average suppleness and range of motion, but more important, a nervous system that allowed his body to move quickly.

Every era in modern golf has had a "king of the hill," one player who stood out above the rest when it came to long driving. Today it is too close to call between Tiger Woods, John Daly, and Davis Love III. But nobody dominated the field like George Bayer did in the 1950s and '60s. He single-handedly eliminated the long-drive contests on Tour because indeed there was "no contest." If George was in the field, everyone knew who was going to win. In his first year on tour, 1955, he finished first in 15 of 16 long-drive events. That is an amazing accomplishment considering that a player is given only three balls to hit and frequently doesn't put one in play. George was so successful that after the first year he quit counting his wins. Much of George Bayer's reputation as a big hitter was developed in the heat of tournament competition when long driving had to be accompanied by accurate driving if you were going to win a check. In a round with Jimmy Demaret and Porky Oliver, he left them speechless as he drove the ball onto the green of the Del Rio Country Club's seventh hole, which was 436 yards long.

Bayer was a varsity football and basketball player at the University of Washington in Seattle and also played semipro baseball. At that point in his life, golf was more a hobby than a sport. Nonetheless, with his 6-foot 6-inch, 240-pound frame, he could power the ball out of sight. The driving range operator at the university practice range one day requested that George stop hitting balls, for they were sailing over the fence, 275 yards distant. Bayer asked if he could hit some left-handed. After getting permission George proceeded to knock them out left-handed. He says he can still hit pretty well from the port side.

With his size Bayer developed a high swing arc, which gave him great leverage. Add that to his athletic skill, flexibility, and

strength and you can see why he was the greatest of the long hitters. He gripped the club from a natural arm-hang position and
applied very light pressure so that he wouldn't "choke off" his
arm and hand speed. His suggestion to the majority of players
with whom he played in Pro-Ams was this: "Do some exercising
to stay supple because you can't sit behind a desk all week and
expect to come out and successfully perform an athletic feat like
the golf swing."

Let's return to the discussion of the small man for an interesting example. A few years back Steve Gaydos, now 86 years of age,
was a little-known pro of tough coal miner stock from Johnstown,
Pennsylvania. Gaydos was only 5 feet 5 inches and weighed 135
pounds, yet imagine this: no takers appeared for his 10-dollar bet
that he could drive the 430-yard first hole at Sunnehanna Golf
Club in Pennsylvania. He once hit a driver and a three-iron on a
560-yard uphill par-five when on the same hole the immortal long
hitter Jimmy Thomson was short with two drivers, with the second shot teed in the fairway. With such a small stature, how could
Gaydos hit it so far? Steve could chin himself by holding onto a
bar with his two little fingers, an unheard-of feat. Great flexibility,
coupled with his abnormal strength, allowed him to accentuate the
well-timed delayed hit, which he employed to explode into the
ball. Steve today recommends a golfer take some rail "to exercise
with." When I asked him, "What do you mean by *rail?*" he
replied, "railroad track, cut up into pieces four to eight inches long
that you use to develop strong hands and forearms." Gaydos held,
rotated, flexed, and extended the rail for stronger muscles. So
strength has something to do with it.

One of the current long-hitting young Tour players we've mentioned, Davis Love III, won the 1997 PGA Championship. He doesn't
wish to be known just as a long hitter. Love has averaged 300
yards for the driver, 275 yards for the three-wood, and 250 yards
for the one-iron. That's right—averaged.

He is not muscularly powerful and weighs about 180 pounds
on a 6-foot 3-inch frame. But he has developed an exceptionally
wide arc on both sides of the ball and employs a move that almost
every long hitter has used in his swing: the increased cocking of

The principle of the late hit, technically called the *conservation of angular momentum*, is demonstrated here. You should have the sensation of retaining the loading action as long as possible before letting it fire.

the wrists in the forward swing. In this move the angle formed by the left arm and clubshaft, using the inside angle, actually decreases as the player starts the forward motion toward the ball. It's called by some *downcocking,* which in effect parallels the archery move of further drawing the bowstring for greater power.

Love developed this move by working on drills with his father, PGA professional Davis Love II, an excellent teacher. They worked very hard on developing the best possible technique; the distance came as a result. Father would make son hit drives 100, 150, and 200 yards while working only on form. When the form was

Every long hitter attempts
to get a powerful windup,
the club in a wide arc, and
a length of backswing to at
least have the shaft reach
parallel to the ground.
Here, the author, at age 62,
demonstrates the value of
physical training.

perfected, Davis III could hit as hard as he wanted provided that
he maintained his form.

John Daly exploits the concept known as the "X Factor," or
the differential in degrees between the shoulder turn and the hip
turn; the larger the number, the better. He has a powerful trunk
like Fred Couples and holds nothing back. Tiger Woods employs
an excellent coil of upper body over the lower, then explodes with
amazing trunk rotation speed with what I call "the fastest hips in
the West."

Perhaps the most impressive of all the long drivers in the world today is the oldest living member of The 350 Club. I purposefully excluded him from the previous chapter because he is different and deserves special attention. Mike Austin is old enough to be a grandfather to most of those in the Club, yet he competed until age 75 and was always a sure bet to drill the ball past the 300-yard markers to open a 350 Club show. At an outing in Japan, he averaged 318 yards for six balls, and that was at 74 years of age. Austin once toured 39 states, offering 10,000 dollars to any man who could outdrive him. There were no winners.

The Guinness Book of World Records lists Mike Austin as having driven 65 yards beyond the 450-yard hole at Wildwood Golf Course in Las Vegas, which adds up to an official 515 yards! That is documented. At age 71, he won the local qualifier for the National Long Drive Contest with a poke of 360 yards. Do you realize how far most 71-year-olds hit the ball? How did he do it? Well, the first answer is technique. One of his fans said, "Mike Austin was classic in his swing. Such perfect flowing power, you can't see where he gets it. He'd make silky Larry Mize's swing look jerky." Austin was no average senior citizen retiree, sitting in a lounge chair watching television, eating and drinking too much, and riding a cart every time he set foot on a golf course. At 75 he was a 6-foot 1-inch, 205-pound, physically fit human being who would play nearly to a zero handicap. He trained religiously, concentrating on Hatha yoga and practicing a sound nutritional regime of eating vegetables (two from above the ground and two from below the ground each day), fruits, fish, only occasional meat, and little milk or cheese products. As I write about him, Austin is 88 and still preaching the lifestyle of an athlete, which has always been his secret.

WHAT SHOULD YOU DO?

Could it be any more obvious? To hit a golf ball a long way you must have something or some things going for you—strength,

Good technique will always result in good balance.

flexibility, body lever lengths, technique, or a good nervous system. If you are not blessed with one or more of these attributes, don't expect to win the local long-drive contest.

The promising message contained in this book is that if you do wish to add distance to your shots, you can—providing you are willing to work. While we have yet to find exercises or drills specific to golf for improvement of the nervous system, we know that traits like reaction time can be improved by training.

You have been given several strength-development recommendations that are focused on golf. Strength, particularly that which is specific to golf, *is* a key factor in distance. We have also tried to impress upon you that flexibility is far more important than you might think. Those who have strength need flexibility to create a full, freewheeling motion. Without it, strength is of little value. Good swing technique is probably the most important. But again, one needs a certain degree of strength and better-than-average flexibility to make a truly good golf swing. Your lever lengths (arm, leg, shoulder, girdle) cannot be changed; however, better technique and a longer club can give you a wider arc and a longer drive. Your swing may provide more distance if you have a smooth, unhurried tempo.

Wild, reckless length is unproductive in the scoring column. But to have power and to be able to use it judiciously is a great advantage. For those of you in the majority who just want to reach some more par-fours in two or hit middle and short irons rather than fairway woods, why not go for it? Make the effort. Start a program of improvement and enjoy the results. Don't try to do it alone. If you have not been taught by a professional teacher of golf thus far in your career, I suggest that you seriously consider doing so. Find a professional that has the respect of his or her pupils and a busy lesson schedule, then make a commitment. Don't be impatient and demand instant results. Couple that with a knowledgeable golf fitness trainer and you have a winning combination.

The trained eye of a PGA professional watching over your swing can pick up the minor flaws that may be causing a power leak.

Whatever your circumstance, know this: you can increase the distance you hit a golf ball. You simply have to know what to do and be willing to work at it. Now that you know what to do, the rest is up to you.

So, establish your priorities and goals, work hard toward their achievement, be patient with your progress, accept your limitations, and apply your new power judiciously. And, as is to be expected, the traditional final exhortation: "You can be better than you are by doing what is suggested in this book, and being better than we are at present is what it's all about."

Index

Adams Golf, 102
Adductor-abductor, 69,
    illus. 70
Aim and setup, 21
Alignment, illus. 28
Alignment, square, illus. 29
Anderson, Darryl, 143, 145
Approach, illus. 52
Arc, width of, illus. 31
Arm press, 66
Armour, Tommy, viii
Austin, Mike, 159

Back extension, illus. 67
Back muscles, 73
Back stretch, illus. 123
Backswing, fast, 58
Backswing, too slow, 32
Backswing, unhurried, illus. 30
Balance, 35, illus. 160
Balata, 107
Ball, four-piece, 107
Ball, multicentered, 107
Ball, multicovered, 107
Ball, placement in stance, 27
Ball position, 22, 27
Ball, solid, 107
Ball, two-piece, 107
Ball, wound, 107
Bates, Faye, 28
Bathroom exercises, 82
Bayer, George, vii, 115, 139,
    155
"Behind the back wrist cock-
    ing," illus. 78
Bench press, 66
Biceps curls, 66
"Big Bertha," 104
"Blocked out," 94
Body rotation, illus. 123
Bridgland, Sir Ainsley, 1

Cable pulls, 69
Calisthenics, 63
Callaway driver, 145
Callaway Golf, 104
Casting, 154
Chest press, 66
Clubface, closed, 100
Cochran, Alistair, 2
Coming off the ball, 49
Compression, ball, 108
Connection, 8
Conservation of angular
    momentum, 157, illus. 157
Couples, Fred, 94, 158
Course conditions, 133
Crunch Golf titanium
    head, 145

Daly, John, 155
Dargie Golf, 144
Davies, Laura, 116

DeCandia, Scott, 142
Deceleration, illus. 45
Del Rio Country Club, 155
Delayed hit, 154
Demaret, Jimmy, 155
Dimples, large, 107
Dimples, shallow, 107
Dimples, small, 107
Dispersion factor, 110
"Distance Builder," 63, 73, 80,
    illus. 74
Divot, 98
Downcocking, 157
Drag, 131
Draw, 152
Driver shaft with no clubhead,
    80, illus. 81
Driving practice, 121
Dunaway, Mike, 140
Dunn, Cotton, 119
Dynamic balance, 8

Els, Ernie, 36
Equipment, 97
Exercises, general, 91
    back scratch, illus. 84
    built-in, 91
    leg-overs, illus. 91
    on the road, 91
    side bends, illus. 84

Face angle, 100
Face depth, 102
Face position
    closed, illus. 37
    open, illus. 37
    square, illus. 37
Face progression, 103
Facing, 103
Faldo, Nick, 20
Finish, 57, illus. 125
Finish, balanced, illus. 33
Fister, Sean "The Beast," 100,
    143, 144
Flexibility, 61, 62, 89, 152
Flexibility exercises, 89
Flick, Jim, 1
Flier, 135
Fogg, Henry, 118
Follow-through, 55,
    illus. 56
Forcum, Terry, 142
Forward swing, too early,
    illus. 44
Foundations of a power golf
    swing, 11
Franks, Andy "Ball Park,"
    140, 142

Gamber, Clarence, 116
Gaydos, Steve, 156
Gloves, 135
Gloves, wet weather, 135
Golf Society of Britain, 2
Grip, 10, 12, 13, 19, 20
Grip, changes in, 138
Grip, left-hand, illus. 21

Grip, proper, 12
    baseball, illus. 20
    crosshanded, 10
    full-fingered, 20
    interlocking, illus. 20
    overlapping, illus. 20
    ten-fingered, illus. 20
    three-knuckle, 10
    two-knuckle, 10
"Grip Squeezer," 87
Grip, tightening of, 57
Guinness Book of World
    Records, 159

Hamilton, Bob, 106
Hand exercise gripper, 63,
    illus. 46
Hands, positions of, 12
Hands, unity of, 15
Harbert, Melvin D.
    "Chick," 139
Haydon, T. A. V., 114
Hinging, 17
Hinkle, Lon, 141, 142
Hit, center face, 59
Hit, off-center, 59
Hitting from the top,
    illus. 46
Hitting zone, 42
Hogan, Ben, viii
Hook, 12, 15, 27
Hooper, Michael, 145
"Human Factors Influencing
    the Golf Drive for
    Distance," vii

Impact, 8, illus. 41
"Iron Byron," 109

Jogging, 86
Jones, Ernest, 32
Jones, Robert T., Jr., 103

Kite, Tom, 36

Laidlay, J. E., 12
Lat machine, 68
Late hit, 157
Launch angle, 110
Law, speed, 9
Law, squareness, 9
Laws, 2
Laws, ball flight, 4
Leadbetter, David, 146
Learning aid, illus. 54
Left-side pulling, 43
Leg curls, 68
Leg extension, 68
Leg press, 68
Lehman, Tom, 36
Length of arc, 7
Lever system, 7
Lie angle, 101
Lift, 131
Long Drivers of America, 145
Long Drivers of America,
    observations from, 146

Long, Geoff, 142
Love, Davis, III, 36, 120,
    156, 158

Mallon, Bill, 61
Maynard, Jim, 143
McCarron, Scott, 120
McComish, John, 141, 142
McDermott, Johnny, 117
Mechanical driving machine,
    108, 109
Mental cues, 42
Mickelson, Phil, 13, 34
Middle iron shot, illus. 23, 24
Military press, 66
Miller, Frank, 143
Miller, Johnny, 20
Mitera, Bob, 114
Moment of truth, 56
Muscle memory, 18
Muscles, abdominal, 71,
    illus. 72

National Long Drive
    Competition, viii
Nelson, Byron, 43, 109
Nicklaus, Jack, 115
Nightingale-Conant Corp., 87
Nike Tour, 138
"No-Ball" warmup, 121,
    illus. 122

Oliver, Porky, 155
Over-the-shoulder wrist cock-
    ing, illus. 76
Overload, 63

Palmer, Arnold, 20
Parnevik, Jesper, 94
Paulet, Brian, 143, 145
Paulson, Dennis, 141, 143
Pavin, Corey, 36
Penick, Harvey, 22
PGA Championship, 1944, 106
PGA Master Professional, vii
PGA Professional, 162
PGA Tour, 138, 140
Picard, Henry, 13
Player, Gary, v
"Power Path," illus. 129
Power Swing Fan, illus. 54
Preferences, 3, 8
Pressure, light, 10
Pressure, strong, 10
Price, Nick, 36
Principles, 3
Priorities, 88
Priority, 88
Priority, three levels of, 3
Pronations, 80, illus. 92

Rain, 133
Rainsuit, 134
Range of motion, 89
Ray, Ted, 116, 117

"Reach for the Sky," illus. 85
"Ready-Aim-Flier," 96
Release, 7, 49
Release position, illus. 53
RE/MAX Corporation, 146
Reynolds Metals, 106
Rhythm, 32
Right elbow, illus. 52
"Right elbow to pocket," 43
Rise on toes, 73
Robie, Marie, 115
Rodriguez, Juan "Chi Chi,"
    viii, 155

Sarazen, Gene, 13
Scheinblum, Monte, 143
Search for the Perfect Swing, 2
Sequence of motion, illus. 150
Setup, illus. 150
Setup, chipping and putting,
    53, 54
Shaft, Harrison, 146
Shaft line, illus. 48
Shaft materials, 103
"Shaking Hands" position, 51
Shift, reverse weight, illus. 30
Shift toward target, illus. 40
"Shot-maker," 131
Shoulder flexibility, illus. 128
Side bends, 73
"Slow Back," 130
Sluman, Jeff, 36
Smith, Alec, 117
Smithson, W., 114
Smothering, 27
Snead, Sam, 33, 139
Soling, driver, 101
Souchak, Mike, 139
Souza, Randy, 142
Square hitting, 58
Squarely hit ball, 57
Squareness to the line, 22
Standing too close, illus. 25
Standing too far, illus. 26
"Staying behind the ball," 49
Stewart, Tom, 103
Stobbs, John, 2
Strange, Curtis, 11
Strength, 62, 152, 161
Strength, hand and arm, 91
Sunnehanna Golf Club, 156
Supination, illus. 92
Sweet spot, 58
Swing center, illus. 22
Swing rhythm, 34
Swing weight, 101
Swinging hit, 47
"Swing-o-Meter," illus. 117

Takeaway, inside, 19
Takeaway, outside, 19
Taylor, Dawson, xi
Taylor, John Henry "J. H.," 12
Taylor Made, 144
Teacher, professional, 136

Teachers, golf, 137
Testing balls and clubs, 108
Thomas, Frank, 132
Thomson, Kimmy, 116,
    139, 156
Tight Lies clubs, 102
Timing, 7
Titanium clubheads, 104, 105
Toe Grab, illus. 85
Top of the swing, 47
Toski, Bob, 1
Training and exercises, 61
Training program, my
    personal, 61, 90
Trajectory, lower, 136
Transition from the top,
    illus. 47
Transition move, illus. 38
Trevino, Lee, 94
Triceps press, 66
"Trying to make a golf
    shot," 58
Turn, thighs. 126, 127
Turn, shoulder, 142
Two-lever system, 9

United States Golf
    Association, 26
Upper body, 26

Vardon grip, 13, 18,
    illus. 19
Vardon, Harry, 12, 18, 117
"V"s of the grip, 12, 14

Wall touch, illus. 86
Watson, Tom, 20
Wedge, illus. 35
Weight-shift drill, 27
Weight training, 63
Weighting of the clubhead, 102
Wheelas, Kyle, 113
Williams, Evan, 119, 120, 142
Wilson, Bobby, 145
Winchester, "Wedgy," 142, 146
Wind, 136
Windup, strong, illus. 39
Winrow, Tom, 140
Wiren, Gary, v, vii, 120
Woods, Tiger, 115, 116, 120,
    154, 155, 158
Workout, fitness center, 65
Workout week, 64
Wright, Mickey, 116
Wrist, arched, 29
Wrist builder, illus. 92
Wrist, cupped, 29

Yonex Super ADX head, 145
Yoga, 159

Zaharias, Mildred "Babe"
    Didrikson, 115
Zoeller, Fuzzy, 94
Zuback, Jason, 146